Differentiating by Student Interest

Practical Lessons and Strategies

Joni Turville

EYE ON EDUCATION
6 DEPOT WAY WEST, SUITE 106
LARCHMONT, NY 10538
(914) 833–0551
(914) 833–0761 fax
www.eyeoneducation.com

Library of Congress Cataloging-in-Publication Data

Turville, Joni.
    Differentiating by student interest : practical lessons and strategies / by Joni Turville.
        p. cm.
    Includes bibliographical references and index.
    ISBN 1-59667-047-9
    1. Individualized instruction. 2. Lesson planning. I. Title.
LB1031.T874 2007
371.39′43—dc22

                                                          2007002427

10 9 8 7 6 5 4 3 2

Editorial and production services provided by
Richard H. Adin Freelance Editorial Services
52 Oakwood Blvd., Poughkeepsie, NY 12603-4112
(845-471-3566)

Also Available from EYE ON EDUCATION

Differentiated Instruction:
A Guide for Elementary Teachers
Amy Benjamin

Active Literacy Across the Curriculum:
Strategies for Reading, Writing, Speaking, and Listening
Heidi Hayes Jacobs

Using Data to Improve Student Learning in Elementary Schools
Victoria L. Bernhardt

What Great Teachers Do Differently:
14 Things that Matter Most
Todd Whitaker

Seven Simple Secrets: What the Best Teachers Know and Do
Annette Breaux and Todd Whitaker

Family Math Night: Math Standards in Action
Jennifer Taylor-Cox

Classroom Motivation From A to Z:
How to Engage Your Students in Learning
Barbara R. Blackburn

Classroom Instruction From A to Z:
How To Promote Student Learning
Barbara R. Blackburn

Teach Me—I Dare You!
Judith Allen Brough, Sherrel Bergmann, and Larry C. Holt

How to Reach and Teach ALL Students: Simplified
By Elizabeth Breaux

Classroom Management:
Simplified
Elizabeth Breaux

Improving Your Elementary School: Ten Aligned Steps
for Administrators, Teams, Teachers, Families, and Students
Leslie Walker Wilson

For my children, Brock and Brittany.

Thank you for bringing joy and laughter into my life every day.

Meet the Author

Joni Turville is the Coordinator for the Alberta Initiative School Improvement program in St. Albert, Alberta, Canada. She has taught a wide range of subjects, including special education and technology, at the elementary, secondary, and university levels. For the past several years she has worked in district administration, working with K–12 teachers. Joni has also been involved in consulting on various topics, particularly educational technology and differentiated instruction. She frequently presents across the United States and Canada.

Acknowledgments

Thanks to my friends and colleagues, Lois Gluck, Val Olekshy, and Marg Hansen, who were my peer review team. Your valuable input helped me ensure that these ideas would excite teachers and really be used with their students. Many thanks also to reviewers Connie Erickson, Teresa Tulipana, and Cathie West and to Bob Sickles for believing in this project. Finally, my thanks and admiration goes to my colleagues everywhere. Teaching is an incredibly demanding profession, but it's one of the most important…one in which we have an opportunity to have an impact on children's lives forever. I am grateful to all of you who spend your days with our most precious resource.

Free Downloads

Beginning on page 127, you'll find 34 Blackline Masters. Book buyers have permission to print out these Adobe Acrobat © documents and duplicate them to distribute to your students.

You can access these downloads by visiting Eye On Education's website: www.eyeoneducation.com. Click on FREE Downloads or search or browse our website to find this book and then scroll down for downloading instructions.

You'll need your book-buyer access code: **DIFFIN-7047-9**

Table of Contents

1

Differentiating by Interest

What we want to see is the child in pursuit of knowledge, and not knowledge in pursuit of the child.

—George Bernard Shaw

I can't believe I gave birth to a son who does not like to read. I am an avid reader, and from the time he was a baby, I'd sit him on my knee and I'd read (and he'd chew) books. He loved to listen to stories through his early years, but something happened in elementary school. He began to dislike reading. What's worse, he started to dread reading, when each month, he had to read a book and write a summary.

The regular book report began to be something we both dreaded. It usually involved prodding, poking, and sometimes tears (mostly mine) to get it finished. In late elementary school, one of his teachers had a great idea. She gave the children only three reports to complete during the year. She had a list of presentation ideas, organized by learning style, from which they could choose to present their book. Having three book reports rather than ten was a relief in itself, and then having him be able to choose how he would represent the book was immediately engaging for him. I remember that for his first book, he read one of the huge *Harry Potter* books, and ended up choosing an option that allowed him to dress up as a character and prepare a short monologue. It seemed that knowing that he had some choice in representing his book reduced some of his reluctance to complete the activity. It was interesting for me, as a parent, to see how much more engaging it was for my child when he was provided with choices.

Starting Small with Differentiation

Observing how students in my classroom also became more engaged when given choices started me on the road to learning more about differentiating by interest. Differentiated instruction (DI) as an entire body of work can be a bit intimidating; however, using interest is an easy place to begin. Looking at just one piece of DI, differentiating by interest, provides a way to start small.

Why All the Confusion about Differentiated Instruction?

There seems to be confusion about what DI is and isn't. There can be several reasons for this:

- ♦ It is a philosophy—a way of thinking about teaching and learning, and as such, it is difficult to define and quantify.
- ♦ It encompasses many different fields such as multiple intelligences, brain research, and cooperative learning.

- The research on DI is fairly new. There are not many studies on DI as a whole, but research on components of DI, such as multiple intelligences and cooperative learning, have been around for many years.

- It takes time and experimentation to develop a personal set of beliefs and philosophies that eventually become second nature in building engaging learning opportunities for students.

The Fit of Differentiating by Interest Within a Differentiated Instruction Model

There are many models and conceptualizations of DI, and it is useful if teachers use some type of framework so that planning for differentiation occurs in an effective, strategic way. One framework, developed by Carol Ann Tomlinson of the University of Virginia (Figure 1.1), is represented in a graphic format:

Figure 1.1. Differentiated Instruction Model

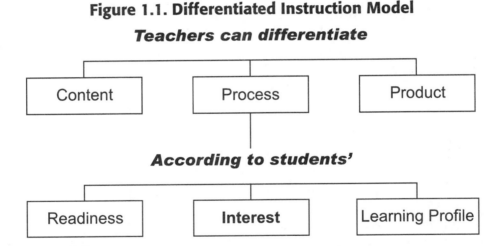

(Tomlinson, 2001)

Teachers can differentiate, or alter the *what* (content), the *how* (process) or the demonstration of understanding (product). The way to decide what to differentiate, or indeed if it is necessary to make these adaptations, depends on the readiness, interest, and learning profiles and preferences of each group of learners. Once these decisions are made, the teacher employs strategies to meet student needs often with strategic grouping of students. Differentiating by interest uses students' situational and personal interests to create choices to optimize engagement and learning.

Looking at this conceptualization of DI, it is apparent that differentiating by interest flows from understanding students, which is the focus of Chapter 2. It is also only one component of differentiation and would not be the only way a teacher would adjust instruction. It is, however, a good place to start.

What Does the Research Say?

In addition to what we know works in practice, there has also been research to support the link between interest and student motivation. It has been suggested that "interest is a doorway to learning" (Tomlinson & Demirsky Allan, 2000, p. 19). This is certainly not a new idea, as evidenced by John Dewey's book *Interest and Effort in Education*, which was published in 1913. In it he very clearly and eloquently talks about how we must engage student interest to help students learn effectively.

Personal and Situational Interest

Researchers describe two different types of interest—situational and personal (Bergin, 1999; Schraw, Flowerday, & Lehman, 2001). Situational interest arises out of something that grabs the learner's attention. Some factors that influence situational interest include the use of humor, novelty, social interaction, and hands-on activities (Bergin, 1999).

Personal interest is something about which a student is internally motivated to learn. It makes sense that students like to learn about things in which they are already personally interested or are related to some goal they have for themselves. Interest can also exist when students have some knowledge in an area, but perceive that there is some gap between what they know and a larger body of knowledge. Teachers can choose activities that address both types of interest. Choices that create either situational interest or personal interest can be provided within a lesson or unit of study.

Linking Interest and Motivation

Some of the research speaks to the link between interest and motivation. In studies where researchers observed students who were offered a choice of activities, it was found that by offering choices, they felt less external control and more intrinsic motivation (Ishee, 2005; Stone, 1995). Along with this increase in motivation, there also appears to be fewer discipline problems and off-task behaviors when students are able to work on topics of interest (Ediger, 2005; Mandel Morrow, 2004). One study states that "giving students the choice and responsibility for selecting something that would further their own education was a powerful, motivating force, indicating respect for the learner" (Todd, 1995, p. 77). It goes on to suggest that perhaps teachers have been focusing on students' willingness (or lack of willingness) to work, instead of focusing on the appropriate tools to motivate them, such as independent study. Research shows that interest and motivation are closely linked.

Overcoming Barriers

Some studies describe that by allowing students to make choices empowers them as learners, and enables them to work more quickly and efficiently through their work (Lause, 2004; Mandel Morrow, 2004) even when it is more challenging (Kohn, 1993; Lause, 2004). Having a level of curiosity or relevance about a topic can help learners to persist through difficult tasks (Alexander, Kulikowich, & Jetton, 1994). We also know that having students work on the cutting edge—where tasks are a little difficult, but where they have support to meeting the challenge, will lead to optimal learning (Brophy, 1999; Tomlinson, 2004).

Interest and Empowerment

Offering interest choices creates a sense of empowerment for students. A number of studies confirm that allowing for student interest choices creates autonomy and self-determination (Deci, Vallerand, Pelletier, & Ryan, 1991; Ishee, 2005; Stone, 1995). A study involving the use of choice in science suggests that teachers be open to having students suggest and choose topics of interest within a unit of study. It states, "Encouraging such student participation and involvement also stimulates the entire class to be more excited about scientific subjects" (Ediger, 2005, p. 17). A 1995 study by Stone suggested that students who feel empowered become independent, thoughtful, creative risks takers. She goes on to state that "empowerment releases the bonds of failure and frees children to go on learning" (p. 296). Students who feel a sense of confidence in one area will be more likely to take learning risks in other areas. The reverse is also true. One author states, "...much of what is disturbing about students' attitudes and behavior may be a function of the fact that they have little to say about what happens to them all day." He goes on to state, "deprive them of self-determination and you have likely deprived them of motivation" (Kohn, 1993, p. 11).

Differentiating in a Standards-Based Climate

Teachers may wonder how it is possible to use a differentiated approach when there is such an emphasis on standards and achievement testing. In fact, they are very compatible. A differentiated lesson should be linked directly to standards and essential understandings and will provide different ways for students to learn these important concepts. This approach will enable students to do better on mandated tests. According to Wormeli (2005):

> [D]ifferentiated instruction and standardized tests are not oxymoronic. Some principals think that if teachers differentiate in their classes, students will be disabled when they take state assessments that are not differentiated. Nothing could be farther from the truth. Students will do well on standardized assessments if they know the materials well, and differentiated instruction's bottom line is to teach in whatever way students learn best. (Wormeli, 2005, p. 29)

Role of the Teacher

Effective teachers show a genuine interest in who their students are as people, and they celebrate individuality. They understand and assess for prior knowledge and student interest (Alexander, Kulikowich, & Jetton, 1994). They also allow students to participate in learning decisions (Strong, Silver, Perini, & Tuculescu, 2003; Stronge, 2002). To provide meaningful interest choices, teachers need to first of all be clear on what the learning goals are. These learning goals must also be evident to students (Brophy, 1999; Scherer, 2002; Strong et al., 2003). Next, the teacher must find activities that will stimulate personal or situational interest. Finally, the teacher must balance differentiation in all ways (in content, process and product—through readiness, interest, and learning profiles) in a strategic way. Once this is achieved, differentiation is effective for all students.

Special Needs Students

The differentiated instruction movement had its roots in gifted education. Carol Ann Tomlinson, a prolific writer on DI, had her teaching roots in gifted and talented education. Many of the principles of helping gifted students become motivated, self-directed learners are just good teaching strategies that should be used with all students. In adjusting instruction, and providing a range of options through flexible grouping, a wide range of student needs can be met. It may, however, still be necessary to make further modifications and adaptations to differentiated lessons for special needs students.

Summary

One researcher suggests that if we teach students to read and write well but end up with students who have no desire to learn, not much has been accomplished. Instead, the goal should be to nurture skills and desire to learn at the same time (Mandel Morrow, 2004). Creating a vibrant classroom learning community is no small feat, but one to which we should aspire. If we truly set the goal of creating lifelong learners, offering interest choices appears to be one way of doing just that.

Linking Interest and Student Achievement

Having teachers integrate new practices requires that they be convinced that trying something new is going to help students in a way that is more effective than what they currently do. Change takes effort and time, and if students do not see the benefits, teachers are often reluctant to adjust practice. How can we make the leap to improved achievement?

Anecdotally, I believe that we can, especially if we reflect back on our own learning experiences. I remember that as a teenager, many of my friends already knew how to downhill ski and I hadn't tried it but wanted to learn. We had a school ski club opportunity where we could take lessons after school and then have some free skiing time. I was very motivated to learn to ski, and as a result, listened intently during the lessons and practiced until I was dragged back onto the bus for the trip home. My main motivation at the time was that I couldn't be with my friends on the harder ski runs until I became more confident and competent, but it didn't take me long until I was keeping up with them. I believe that my interest in learning to ski was a motivator, and as a result, I learned as much as I could and worked hard to achieve the results I wanted.

I have seen similar results with students in the classroom. If students are interested, their level of motivation to learn is increased. As they attend to the learning activities, they become more confident and competent with concepts and skills.

Tying Things Together

Chapter 1 has provided background, research, and anecdotal information about differentiated instruction and differentiating by interest. It has also shown where providing interest options can fit into a DI model. Next, we'll look at how to assess interest and build a classroom climate that supports differentiation.

For Further Reflection

1. How do I plan for differentiation? Does it help me differentiate in a systematic way?
2. How does the research that has been done on interest and motivation support my experiences with students in the classroom?
3. What personal learning experience have I had that would demonstrate a link between interest, motivation and achievement?

2

Assessing Interest and Building Classroom Climate

Imagine what a harmonious world it could be if every single person, both young and old, shared a little of what he is good at doing.

—Quincy Jones

Creating a caring, respectful learning environment is an essential component in creating a successful differentiated classroom. Students must feel that they are in a safe environment where their uniqueness will be respected. In today's society, it seems that children feel the pressure to conform at a younger and younger age, so teachers need to make conscious efforts to celebrate differences.

Assessing Interest

There are many techniques and tools that can be used to assess student interests. Students who are very verbal and confident will often talk about themselves, what interests them, and how they spend their time outside of school. Other students, however, will be reluctant to share information about themselves. Using a variety of techniques can help teachers get to know all their students, including those who are more hesitant to share.

One teacher related a story about a student at her school. The boy was very quiet, and didn't often share about his after-school activities. It wasn't until he was ready to leave the school that she found out that he was a national-level karate champion. She felt that she could have asked him to share his expertise, celebrate his successes, and encourage him to integrate his special skills into his work if she had known about his accomplishments.

There are many different ways to uncover student interests, and Chapter 2 will outline some of these techniques, as well as provide sample tools.

Interest Inventories

Interest inventories are an effective tool to determine student interests and preferences. They can be completed independently by students who are able to read and write well. For students who are less able to complete these by themselves, the following techniques could also be used:

- ◆ Cross-age partners
- ◆ Parent-volunteer readers and scribes
- ◆ Tape-recorded responses
- ◆ Drawn responses with scribed descriptions
- ◆ Nonverbal interest inventories

In the Blackline Master section are samples of inventories that could be used by a variety of students. There is an interest inventory for primary students (Blackline Master 1) or older students (Blackline Master 2).

Technology Connection

A simple search using terms such as "interest inventory" or "assessing interest" will yield a number of samples that teachers can use if they would like to extend the ideas presented in the Blackline Masters. If you want to have a search engine search for the exact term, search the phrase using quotation marks (e.g., "interest survey" rather than interest survey).

Nonverbal Interest Inventory (Blackline Master 3)

Interest inventories can be made easier for nonwriters, less verbal students or English language learners by using a nonverbal interest inventory (Figure 2.1). Simply have students print their names in the oval in the middle of the page (or have someone help with this step), and then ask them to draw or paste pictures that represent things that interest them. They could be prompted to include such things as hobbies, sports, television programs, games, friends and clubs. To extend this activity, teachers, older students or parent volunteers could write a description underneath each picture after discussing the interests with each student.

Figure 2.1. Nonverbal Interest Inventory

Parent-Completed Interest Inventories

Remember to use parents as a resource to find out more about student interests. Studies have shown the positive impact of parental involvement on student success at school (Nakagawa, 2000; Mattingly, Prislin, McKenzie, Rodriguez, & Kayzar, 2002). Occasionally there are a few children who do not bring such inventories back. In this case the teacher could complete them with the student, or have an older student or volunteer do a one-on-one visit with the student. Blackline Master 4 contains a sample of a parent-completed interest inventory.

Technology Connection

Online surveys are quick and easy ways to collect information. There are a variety of sites, such as formsite.com, surveymonkey.com, and zoomerang.com. They enable online surveys to be created quickly, without any special computer expertise. The benefit to using these tools is that students can work through them in a computer lab, or on a classroom computer, and the teacher has instant, tabulated results. The following is a sample that could be created from such a service:

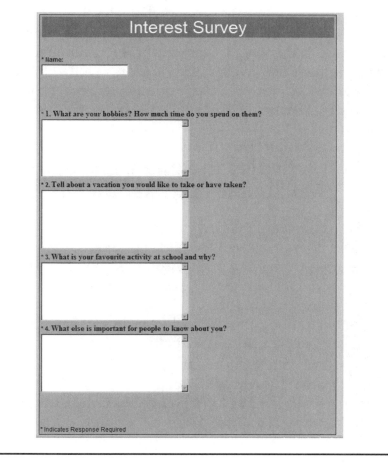

School-Wide Initiatives

Some schools make a concerted effort to recognize interests and hobbies outside of school activities. For example, Ronald Harvey School in St. Albert, Alberta, Canada, found another use for the display case used to house trophies and other such items. During the school year, each classroom takes a turn being featured in the display case. Students are asked to bring something that tells about their interests outside of school. Students bring photos of family hobbies, sports trophies, crafts, among a wide array of objects. Each student (or parent for nonwriters) is asked to write a brief description of the item on display. It allows students to celebrate their outside interests and be recognized for their out-of-school accomplishments.

Other schools have talent shows or use digital photography options to collect images of students engaged in extracurricular and community activities.

Technology Connection

At the beginning of a school year consider having students create a classroom slideshow. Each student creates a slide that tells about himself or herself and his or her interests, including a voice-over description. The slides can be put into a classroom presentation and be looped for the students to get to know each other, for "Meet the Teacher Night," or other times when parents and students are invited to the school. Students love to hear about themselves and their classmates in their own voices. KidPix works well with primary students in this sort of exercise, and Hyperstudio and PowerPoint can be used in similar ways with older students.

Activities to Build a Climate to Support Differentiation

In addition to traditional interest inventories, there are many other activities that can be done to assess interest, as well as build classroom climate. Part of what makes differentiation possible is creating an environment where differences and unique talents are recognized and celebrated. The activities that follow integrate well with a variety of subject areas, such as reading, writing, math, and technology. They are also great to use at the beginning of the school year, but it is most effective if teachers continue to emphasize an accepting classroom climate throughout the school year.

Don't forget to participate in these activities yourself. By sharing your own interests and passions with the students, they get to know you on a personal level. Modeling the sharing of personal interests and unique characteristics also helps to encourage students to follow suit.

The many different ways to build classroom community described here integrate well into a variety of subject areas. A collection of lesson ideas and Blackline Masters follow.

Silhouettes

1. Using a bright light, have a student sit so that his or her facial silhouette is projected onto a piece of paper.

2. In partners, students outline their silhouettes (or older students or parent volunteers could be used).

3. Have them write words around their silhouette that would describe how others see them on the "outside" (Figure 2.2).

4. On the inside of the silhouette, use a white pencil crayon to write words that describe how they feel on the "inside" (their interests and feelings that are internal).

Figure 2.2. Sample Silhouette

Variation: Cut out silhouette. Paste magazine pictures or digital photos that represent personal qualities and interests in a collage over the silhouette. Trim around silhouette and display.

The Treasures of Me

1. Have each student bring in a shoebox or other small box.
2. Ask the students to collect objects, pictures, and so forth, which they can place in the box that would represent their interests, and who they are, as persons.
3. Share with the class.

Note: An assignment note for students can be found on Blackline Master 5.

Hint: Only ask four to six students to share each day, or it can become tedious if done in one session.

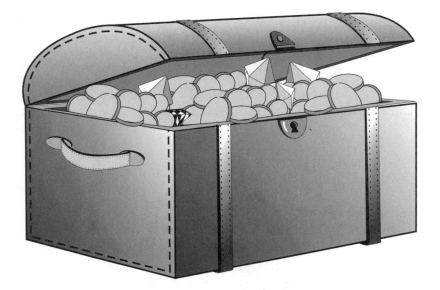

Variation: Ask students to fill the box with artifacts that tell things that others might not know about them (their internal selves), and to decorate the outside of the box with things they think others already know about their interests (their external selves).

Classroom Interest Quilt

1. Discuss personal interests. Read a story, such as *The Patchwork Quilt* by Valerie Flournoy, *Eight Hands Round: A Patchwork Alphabet* by Ann Whitford Paul, or *The Keeping Quilt* by Patricia Polacco.

2. Do a think/pair/share and discuss personal interests and hobbies.

3. Give each student a quilt square and have him or her decorate it with personal interests and hobbies.

4. Join together in a classroom quilt and discuss the importance of having many different kinds of people and interests in making a diverse and strong community of learners (Figure 2.3).

Note: A blank patchwork quilt square can be found on Blackline Master 6

Figure 2.3. Classroom Interest Quilt

Variation: Have students decorate cloth patches with fabric markers, fabric paint, glitter, and so on. Have a parent volunteer sew patches into a real quilt that could be used in a story corner and/or raffled off at the end of the school year.

VIP Venn Diagrams

This activity will allow pairs of students to get to know each other and compare their interests.

1. With younger students, read the book *Being Friends* by Karen Beaumont. This story lends itself well to this task in particular because it compares the likes and dislikes of two characters. The teacher can use this story to discuss and model the completion of a class Venn diagram as a reading comprehension activity. For older students, the teacher could use two volunteers to demonstrate how to complete a Venn diagram comparing two students' interests.

2. Have students interview each other in partners to determine their individual interests.

3. Have them create a large Venn diagram together to share and post on a classroom display (Figure 2.4).

Note: A blank Venn diagram can be found on Blackline Master 7

Figure 2.4. Venn Diagram

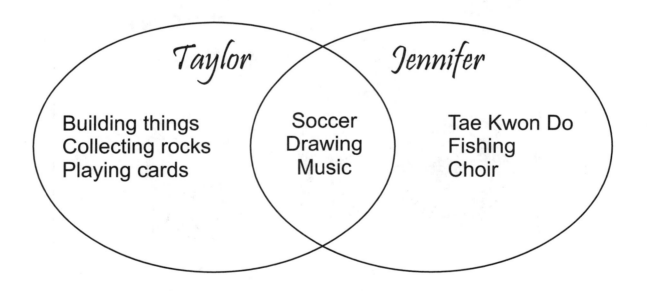

Variation: Use a triple Venn diagram for three students for an extra challenge. A blank triple Venn diagram can be found on Blackline Master 8.

Interest Graphing

Students work in small groups to create a tally of their interests and then create a graph.

1. In small groups, have students discuss their interests (teacher can prompt for in-school favorite activities, out of school favorites, or a combination).
2. Have them list interests and create a tally as they chat.
3. Have them create a graph of their group's interests. They can use a bar graph, pictograph, or a computer-generated graph (Figure 2.5).

Variation: A whole-class bar graph could also be created and used as a display.

Note: A blank bar graph can be found on Blackline Master 9.

Figure 2.5. Interest Graph

Baseball	*Reading*	*Gymnastics*	*Computer*	*Music*	*Dancing*

Group Names:

Hint: The teacher may want to model this with a small group prior to having students work independently.

Technology Connection

Teachers can have students use a spreadsheet or graphing program to create an electronic graph. It could then be manipulated into a variety of graphing formats, such as a pie graph or line graph. If you have an interactive white board in your school, you could consider importing all the data into a single spreadsheet together and then manipulating the data display as a demonstration and a graph that would represent the entire class.

Puzzle Pieces

Students are all given a puzzle piece to create a classroom puzzle that is a metaphor for how a community needs all of its members to be complete.

1. Teacher takes a large piece of stiff paper and draws enough puzzle pieces to create one piece for each student and the teacher(s) in the room.

2. Each student writes his or her name on the puzzle piece and decorates it with images and/or words describing his or her interests (Figure 2.6).

3. Puzzle could be assembled and used as a bulletin board display and/or kept at a center so students could complete the puzzle in their free time.

Variations:

♦ Each student could be given their own small puzzle to complete, illustrating all their interests, or "pieces" of themselves. See Blackline Master 10 for a template.

♦ This technique also works well with real puzzles that are old or inexpensive. Simply spray paint the puzzle with one or two coats of a matte white paint, and students can use felt pens to draw on their each piece.

Figure 2.6. Puzzle Pieces

Important Books

Read *The Important Book* or *Another Important Book* by Margaret Wise Brown. Both books have a very rhythmic quality to them and would be wonderful read-alouds.

Students could use the patterns contained in the books to create their own books about themselves, or they could create one page for a classroom book about what makes each person in the class unique and important (Figure 2.7).

Figure 2.7. Important Book

The most important thing about Brock is that he is funny.

He has red hair and brown eyes.

He knows a lot about weather forecasting.

But the most important thing about Brock is that he is funny.

(Patterned after *The Important Book* by Margaret Wise Brown)

Note: Sample templates can be found on Blackline Masters 11 and 12.

Ish Books/Posters

1. Read the book *Ish* by Peter Reynolds. This story is a reminder that individuality is a gift to be celebrated.
2. Discuss personality traits or personal interests that describe students' lesser-known talents. They might be athletic-ish, musical-ish, and so on.
3. Create posters or drawings of something they are "ish" at (Figure 2.8).
4. A classroom display or book could be created.

Figure 2.8. Ish Poster

I am artistic-ish

Note: Sample template can be found on Blackline Master 13.

Interest Bingo

1. Have students complete a card detailing their interests on a piece of grid paper (see Blackline Master 14).
2. Students can be prompted for interests if they have difficulty filling in their cards, or they can have a minute or two to talk about their interests with partners to help generate ideas.
3. Pass out bingo chips or other markers. Decide how a bingo will be called (e.g., horizontal line, vertical line, four corners, black out).
4. Randomly call on students to name one of their interests.
5. Students cover any interests that match theirs until someone calls a bingo (Figure 2.9).

This game would make a great beginning of the year activity, and the cards could be placed at a free-time center or used as an ongoing classroom activity or a bulletin board display.

Figure 2.9. Interest Bingo

skiing	playing outside with my friends	bike riding
reading	puzzles	writing
listening to music	video games	magic tricks

Tying Things Together

The activities described in this chapter are only some of many you could use to understand student interests to create a classroom climate that will facilitate differentiation. Some of the inventories and activities may be twists on things that are already familiar and some may be new. Taking time to assess student interest and celebrate uniqueness is an essential part of a differentiated classroom.

For Further Reflection

1. What are my current practices for assessing interest and creating a positive, accepting classroom climate?
2. How can I add new ideas or adapt existing ones to continue to create a climate that supports differentiation?
3. How do I plan to share ideas with colleagues and create some school-wide initiatives?
4. How may I continue to recognize and celebrate differences throughout the school year?

3

Lesson Structures that Support Differentiating by Interest

The whole art of teaching is only the art of awakening the natural curiosity of young minds for the purpose of satisfying it afterwards.

—Anatole France

There are many different lesson structures that can be used to differentiate by interest. Some interest lessons will develop situational interest and help students gain enthusiasm for a topic. Others can introduce tasks that would be of interest to students because of prior knowledge, background, or interest in a topic (personal interest). Examples of such structures are choice boards; role, audience, format, and topic projects (RAFTs); cubing; learning contracts; and WebQuests. Chapter 3 will describe each of these lesson structures, as well as provide step-by-step instruction for creating learning opportunities that differentiate instruction and support student learning.

Being Specific with Learning Outcomes

The first step in creating any differentiated lesson is to make explicit what students should know, understand, and be able to do as a result of the lesson. Diane Heacox (2002) calls these concepts KUDos. If the teacher isn't crystal clear on the learning outcomes, then it's likely that they will be busy doing many activities, but they may or may not end up learning the important concepts. The types of activity structures described in this chapter can take longer than what can be accomplished in a single class, so the teacher must also decide if these activities are worth the students' time and effort. There can also be confusion when connecting to learning outcomes, especially between the *know* and *understand*. The KUDos can be thought of in the following ways:

Know: "Just the facts, ma'am."

The *know* can be thought of as the lower-level items on Bloom's taxonomy, such as *knowledge* , for example, fact recall, definitions, identification, and so forth.

Understand: "What's the big idea?"

The *understand* is equivalent to the higher-level items on Bloom's taxonomy, such as comprehend (e.g., interpret, generalize, summarize, extend), *analysis* (e.g., patterns, organization, meanings, inferences), *synthesis* (e.g., generalizations, relationships, predictions, conclusion), and *evaluation* (e.g., comparisons, assessments, choices, judgements, explanations, summarizations, conclusions). These will be the concepts and principles that should endure beyond the lesson and be transferable to other situations and problems.

Do: "Show what you know."

The *do* is similar to the *application* component on Bloom's taxonomy. This will enable students to show what they understand about the topic at hand, for example, demonstrate, use information, solve problems, modify, examine, and illustrate.

The first place to look when beginning to formulate the KUDos is in curriculum or standards documents. They include outcome statements that teachers may need to clarify and break into smaller chunks.

Blackline Master 15 contains an easy-to-use summary of the KUDos and can serve as a quick reference during lesson planning.

Selecting Learning Activities

When teachers are planning lessons, brainstorming interesting activities for students seems to be something that comes easily. The difficulty of planning to differentiate is taking a critical look at these activities and deciding which activities will lead students to the important outcomes. Often teachers will be adamant that a learning activity be included because it will be fun for students to do. This is not in itself a bad thing, but if its sole purpose is fun, and doesn't clearly link to the learning outcomes, then it should be substituted with a learning activity that does. There never seems to be enough time to cover the curriculum, so learning activities should be selected carefully.

Activity Structures that Can Help to Differentiate Instruction

Choice Boards

Choice boards can take the form of a tic-tac-toe game board, or they can take a shape that compliments the unit of study. They enable students to choose learning activities that are designed by the teacher. Giving students choices in their learning enhances student engagement and increases the opportunity for student success. Researchers have found that allowing choices can create a high level of interest and motivation (Collins & Amabile, 1999).

They can be used in any subject area and be used to differentiate by interest. They enable demonstration of understanding of a topic or concept. They can be created to allow students choices in representing their learning. Teachers can structure these boards in any number of ways, depending on their purpose. See samples, Figures 3.1 and 3.2

They can be designed in many ways:
- With random tasks representing various interests
- By multiple intelligences
- By learning style
- With Bloom's taxonomy

Figure 3.1. My School Community Tic-Tac-Toe

Make a tape recorded interview of someone in your school community. Be sure to have your questions ready before you start the interview.	Collect items from around the school that tell about different people in the school and what they do. Be able to share about what each item represents.	Spend some time following a person in the school to find out what they do. Share this information in a written or oral report.
Create a survey to determine which jobs students think are the most important in the school. Share the results orally or in writing.	Free space! Choose any role in the school and think of a way to show how it contributes to the school community.	Create a newspaper wanted advertisement for a job in the school. Be sure to tell job applicants what kinds of skills they need to do this job.
Create a pantomime of different people in the school that shows some of the jobs that they do.	Take digital pictures or make drawings of different people in your school and create a scrapbook that has a page for each person with a description of what they do.	Create a slogan for a bumper sticker that represents a role and responsibility in your school.

Figure 3.2. Learning About Insects Choice Board

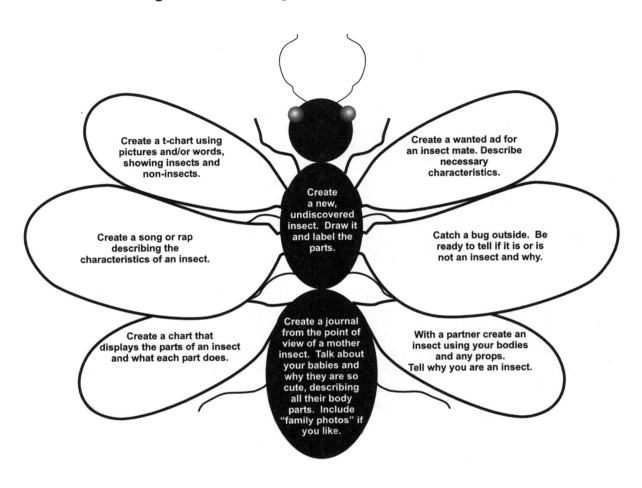

Checklist for Creating a Choice Board

- ☐ Identify the KUDos—What do you want the students to Know, Understand, and Be Able to Do as a result of completing a choice board task?
- ☐ Brainstorm a variety of activities
- ☐ Eliminate tasks that will not lead the students to these KUDos.
- ☐ Decide on what your choice board will look like. Will you create a tic-tac-toe, a list of choices or a structure that matches a theme of study?
- ☐ How will you have students work through these tasks?
  - ❏ Will you have one "core" activity that all students must complete to learn a key concept, and then complete a vertical, horizontal or diagonal line of other activities from there?
  - ❏ Will you have a "free space" "or "free choice" somewhere on the board where students can design their own activity?
- ☐ Choose the activities from your brainstormed list and place onto the board.
- ☐ Decide how the projects will be evaluated.

This checklist can be found on Blackline Master 16.

RAFTs

The acronym RAFT stands for role, audience, format, and topic (Santa, 1988). It was originally used for writing assignments in English language arts. In recent years, it has been adopted by those who are interested in differentiated instruction and can involve products beyond just written work. RAFTs help to differentiate because they provide choices for students and can be written so the choices are engaging for students. They can be particularly effective in helping students explore points of view. Figure 3.3 provides an explanation of each component of a RAFT, and a science example follows (Figure 3.4).

Figure 3.3. RAFT

	Role	*Audience*	*Format*	*Topic*
What it is	Students assume a role that is related in some manner to the task.	Students create the product for an identified person, group, object, etc.	Refers to type of product that will be used to explain the topic to the audience	Refers to the subject or often the title of the piece of work
Examples	• self • character • real-world worker • inanimate object	• self • classmates • parents • animals • inanimate objects	• song • rap • diary entry • letter • chart • flowchart • poem • map • story • model • dramatization	• an attention-grabbing or humorous subject related to the role and audience

Figure 3.4. Animal Life Cycle RAFT

Role	*Audience*	*Format*	*Topic*
Egg	Adults	Poem	I've got potentiality!
Larva	Other Larva	Play	I don't want to grow up
Adult	Larva	Chart	I'm tired of all this responsibility
Pupa	Adults	Song or rap	Please release me, let me go

Checklist for Creating a RAFT Project

☐ Identify the KUDos—What do you want the student(s) to know, understand, and be able to do as a result of completing the RAFT project?

☐ Brainstorm a variety of projects that students could complete (these will become the "formats").

☐ Brainstorm roles, audiences, and topics for each format.

☐ Eliminate the tasks that will not lead students to what you want them to know, understand, and be able to do.

☐ Decide on a reasonable timeline to complete the tasks.

☐ Determine how the project(s) will be evaluated.

☐ Create the RAFT.

Blackline Master 17 shows this checklist.

Tips for creating RAFTs

• You don't necessarily have to have all different roles, audiences, formats, or topics. One or more can remain constant depending on your learning goals.

• Consider involving students in the brainstorming process to create a raft.

• Consider learning preferences, interests, and readiness in the choices.

Cubing

Cubing involves creating a three-dimensional cube that has task choices on it. Each face on the cube describes an activity that students would complete to achieve the learning goals. The activities on the cube can be more generic (Figure 3.5 and Blackline Master 18), or they can be specific to the topic at hand. Cubes are often used at the end of a unit of study when students have a common language and understanding of a topic and then can do projects of interest to them. Cubing can be used to create situational interest because of the novelty of this activity. It is also possible to create more of a personal interest choice by allowing students to roll the cube twice and choose the task that interests them the most.

Checklist for Creating a Cubing Project

☐ Identify the KUDos—What do you want the student(s) to know, understand, and be able to do as a result of completing the cubing activity?

☐ Brainstorm a variety of tasks that students could complete.

☐ Eliminate the tasks that will not lead students to what you want them to know, understand, and be able to do.

☐ Choose the best six activities, so there is one for each face of the cube.

❏ Decide on a reasonable timeline to complete the task.

❏ Determine how the projects will be evaluated.

❏ Create the cube(s) (see Blackline Master 19).

This checklist can be found on Blackline Master 20.

Alternate Suggestions for Making Cubes

If creating the cubes from paper patterns isn't appealing, try these ideas:

♦ Put six numbered choices on a chart and roll a regular die to determine the students' project.

♦ Buy a plastic photo cube and insert tasks into the photo places. Roll on the carpet.

♦ Buy a large, spongy cube or die. Put tasks on laminated task cards and tape to the die.

Figure 3.5. Generic Cube

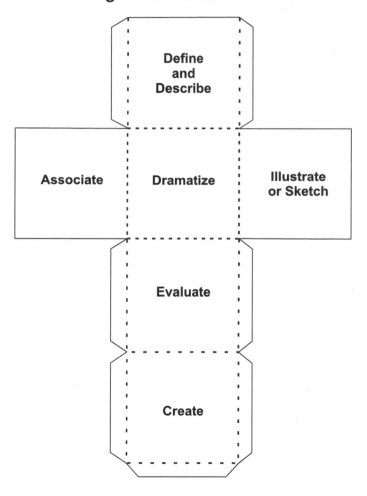

Learning Contracts

Learning contracts are an excellent tool; they allow students choice within a range of specified activities. They are a kind of pact between the teacher and the learner to complete a series of tasks that are designed to achieve specific learning goals. They can be created so that students can work individually on an independent study, in a small interest group or as a whole class. They can be developed by the teacher or jointly by the teacher and students. Most contracts include a place for the date and signatures of the teacher and student (and parents, if desired). This makes it feel like an official contract for the student and helps everyone signify that they understand what is required.

Contracts are beneficial because learners are able to make choices that interest them. They encourage the development of responsibility and time management skills in the learner as they make choices each day to complete the tasks they have chosen by the deadline indicated by the teacher.

Checklist for Creating a Learning Contract

- ☐ Identify KUDos—What do you want the students to know, understand, and be able to do as a result of completing the contract?
- ☐ Brainstorm a variety of tasks the students could complete.
- ☐ Eliminate the tasks that will not lead the students to what you want them to know, understand, and be able to do.
- ☐ Decide on a reasonable timeline to complete the tasks and how many students will be asked to complete.
- ☐ Determine how and the frequency with you will check in with students during their contract work. Make this explicit in the contract.
- ☐ Outline how students will ask for help if needed.
- ☐ List the resources that students are able to use and how they should be cited.
- ☐ Determine how the project(s) will be evaluated. Give the rubrics or other evaluation tools to the students and discuss together before they start the assignment.
- ☐ Write up contract in a businesslike manner (i.e., use precise, formal language). Be sure to include places for dates and signatures.

This checklist can be found on Blackline Master 21.

Technology Connection

Contract Generators

There are a few places on the Web where you can make a contract using an online template. After the question prompts are completed, a contract is generated that could be printed out and given to students. One place on the World Wide Web that has such a service is at Teachnology (http://www. teach-nology.com/web_tools/contract).

WebQuests

WebQuests are an inquiry-based activity where much of the material and information students use is web-based. WebQuests are effective because of their common structure, as well as having teacher-chosen, embedded Web links within each project. Bernie Dodge of the University of San Diego is commonly thought of as the WebQuest guru. His site, WebQuest Page (www.webquest.org), has thousands of hits per day. It contains basic information on WebQuests, and one useful feature is the matrix that shows subject/grade level matches. Teachers could easily go to an upcoming topic of study and have several choices for WebQuests within a single topic.

WebQuests can be used to differentiate by interest in a number of ways. The WebQuests themselves are inquiry-based, and many of them are based on some type of real-world scenario where students are asked to assume a role within a task. Students could choose these roles based on interest. WebQuests are also a great way to have an individual student or group of learners extend their understanding of a topic in doing some independent work. They work particularly well for this purpose because they are so well structured. Teachers must take care that the WebQuests will help meet and extend learning outcomes. Sites such as the WebQuest Page and bestwebquests.com have a rating system so teachers can choose ones that have been reviewed and found to be of high quality. No matter where the WebQuest is located, it is important for teachers to check all the links and make sure they point where they are supposed to, and that there aren't many dead links.

Where to start with WebQuests

- http://bestwebquests.com/—This is a site that has a WebQuest matrix by grade and subjects, and rates them with a star system.

- http://webquest.org/—This is Bernie Dodge's site from the University of San Diego. For basic information, try a WebQuest on WebQuest's http://webquest.sdsu.edu/ webquestwebquest-es.html (elementary version) or http://webquest.sdsu.edu/web questwebquest-hum.html (middle/high school version). There is a great deal of background material here that would be great to use as staff professional development, such as "The Building Blocks of a WebQuest."

- http://www.ozline.com/learning/index.htm—This is another major site with information and links for WebQuests.

- http://www.techtrekers.com/webquests/—This site is sorted by subject, and the WebQuests also have a short annotation so you can get a feel for what each is about.

- http://www.kn.pacbell.com/wired/fil/—Filamentality is an online site where you can create your own WebQuest without having to use HTML. If you can navigate a Web page, you can use this tool.

Creating a WebQuest

Before creating an original WebQuest, check to see if a similar WebQuest already exists. If there isn't an exact match to your standards, it is certainly possible to take an existing WebQuest and adapt the activities for your particular group of students. If nothing is suitable, a WebQuest can be created. They have a similar structure and are focused on inquiry-based ideas (Dodge, 1997). The components are as follows:

Introduction: This part introduces the focus of the project/topic. It often gives a real-life scenario in which students are to engage. The best ones involve a hook so that learners are motivated to begin the WebQuest.

Task: This section outlines the general idea of the task in which students will engage. It should outline the learning outcomes that students will achieve by completing the project.

Process: Step-by-step instructions are described so that students are able to complete the task independently. Handouts, checklists, or guiding questions can be provided.

Evaluation: Evaluation tools and processes are made clear to the students. They should have these criteria prior to beginning the task.

Conclusion: These activities help students bring some closure to the activity and often suggests ways in which project findings can be shared.

The following steps may be helpful in creating a WebQuest:

Checklist for Creating a WebQuest

- ☐ Decide on a subject or topic.
- ☐ Identify the KUDo—What do you want students to know, understand, and be able to do as a result of completing the WebQuest?
- ☐ Brainstorm tasks that would lead students to the important learning outcomes.
- ☐ Eliminate the tasks that will not lead the students to what you want them to know, understand, and be able to do.
- ☐ Search for Web sites that are of an appropriate reading level and contain information that students will need.
- ☐ Choose tasks and Web sites that would most effectively lead students to understanding the important learning outcomes.
- ☐ Decide on an introduction or hook that will engage students in the task.
- ☐ Write guiding questions and step-by-step instructions for each WebQuest section.
- ☐ Determine how students will present or share their information.
- ☐ Decide how student work will be evaluated.

This checklist can be found on Blackline Master 22.

WebQuest Example: The Bowhead Whale Hunting WebQuest

I created this WebQuest for students to study aboriginal populations in the North, and there were issues in the news surrounding the traditional whale hunt because the whales had been deemed endangered. I decided that a WebQuest would be a great way to help students investigate the complexity of this issue and differentiate instruction. It is still an active WebQuest that is featured on both www.webquests.org and www.bestwebquests.com. Figure 3.7 displays a screen shot of the main page, and following it are descriptions of each of the main sections of the WebQuest. The words and phrases titles underlined are live links to Web sites that will help students complete the research needed to answer the questions in each section.

Figure 3.6. Bowhead Whale Hunting WebQuest

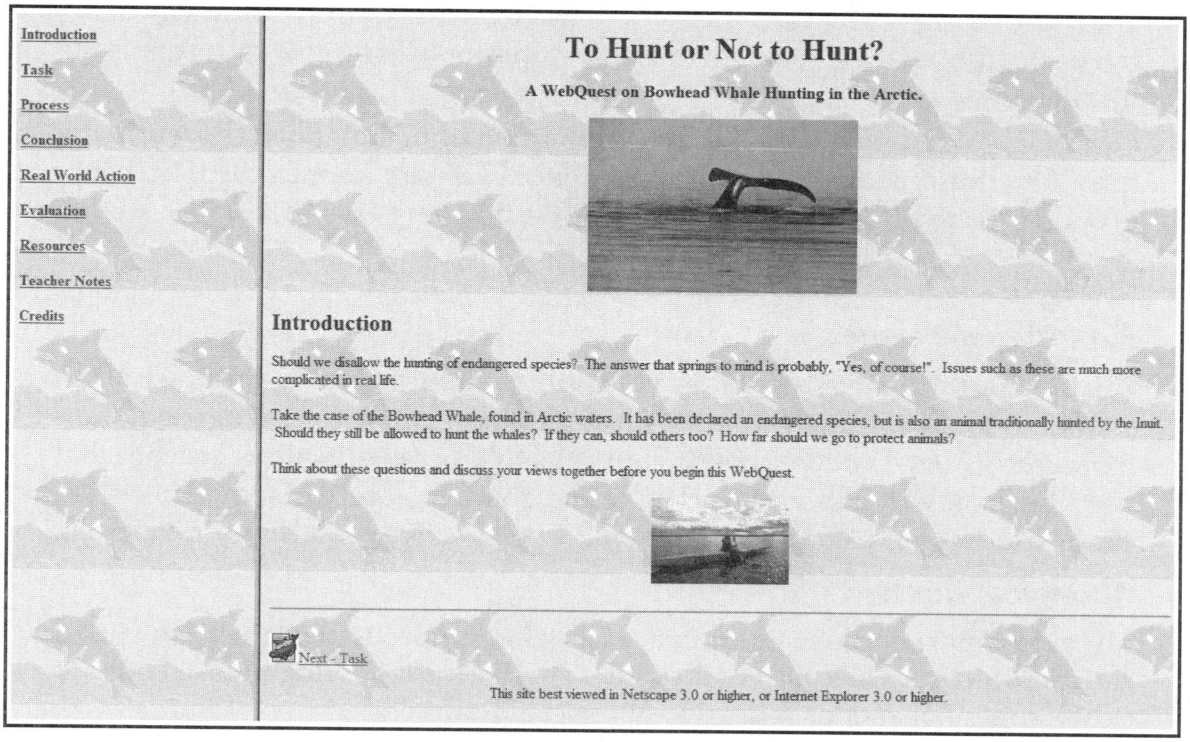

Introduction

Should we disallow the hunting of endangered species? The answer that springs to mind is probably, "Yes, of course!" Issues such as these are much more complicated in real life.

Take the case of the Bowhead whale, found in Arctic waters. It has been declared an endangered species but is also an animal traditionally hunted by aboriginal people. Should they still be allowed to hunt the whales? If they can, should others too? How far should we go to protect animals? Think about these questions and discuss your views together before you begin this WebQuest.

Task

You will work in groups and assume different roles. These cooperative groups will first look at some background information on Bowhead whales, and then information specific to their role.

Your group's task will be to work through the questions posed. You may have other questions that arise from your work in the specified Web sites, and in other resources available in your school and community. Your goal will be to attempt to answer this primary question: Should *all* hunting of Bowhead whales be prohibited?

There are no right or wrong answers to this question or others that will arise, but each group will be asked to form their opinion and be able to give reasons for their view.

Finally, each group will present the information from their point of view in the form of a multimedia presentation. It should contain an introduction, background information, and conclusion with supporting evidence.

Process

Exploring the Issues

For this part of your WebQuest, your group should choose a role. You can choose to be an aboriginal hunter, an environmental protection agent, or animal activist. Once you've chosen your role, follow the directions beneath that heading. You will notice that some of the questions are "biased." This is because you are to explore the issue from the perspective of someone in that role.

Aboriginal Hunter

The aboriginal people have hunted whales for hundreds of years. It isn't just a source of food, it's also part of their culture. Use the following Internet links to explore these questions related to aboriginal hunting:

1. Why do you think culture and tradition are so important to the aboriginal people?
2. Describe a traditional aboriginal whale hunt.
3. How is a whale hunt (and hunting in general) part of the aboriginal culture?
4. How do aboriginal legends relate to the hunting of the Bowhead whales?
5. Why are the aboriginal people allowed to hunt the endangered Bowhead whales?
6. Why do the aboriginal people feel it is important for them to be able to hunt the whales?

Internet Links

♦ Revival of Whale Hunt Sparks Bitter Debate at http://www.whale watch.co.nz/
♦ Traditional Whale Hunting at http://www.usask.ca/education/ideas/tplan/sslp/trad.htm
♦ Whaling—A Way of Life at http://www.alaskool.org/projects/traditionalife/WhalingAWOL/WHALING-English.html

- What other information do you think is important to the aboriginal point-of-view on this topic? Why do you think so?

- Click here if you would like to use a template (available at http://rhem.spschools.org/specialprojects/webquest/inuittemplate. html) to help you in organizing your multimedia presentation.

Animal Protection Activist

As an animal activist, your concern is the humane treatment of animals. Explore the following Internet links and answer these questions:

1. Do you think it is time for the aboriginal to abandon the practice of whale hunting?

2. Why were recent unsuccessful Bowhead whale hunts considered inhumane and unproductive?

3. Does the method the aboriginal people use to hunt cause instant death?

4. Why is it difficult to humanely kill a whale, in some people's opinion?

5. Do you eat meat (beef, chicken, etc.)? Do you think killing animals for food is a good thing to do? Why or why not?

Internet Links

- Permission to Hunt Endangered Whale at http://www.canoe.ca/ AllAboutCanoesNewsMar00/20_whale.html

- Whales—Their Emerging Right to Life at http://anthonydamato.law. northwestern.edu/Papers-1/A911-whales.html

- Save the Whales at http://www.savethewhales.org/

  - What other information do you think is important to the animal protection activist point of view on this topic? Why do you think so?

  - Click here if you would like to use a template to help you in organizing your multimedia presentation.

Environmental Protection Agent

Environmental protection is concerned with the preservation of the whales and the ocean environment in general. Your job is to investigate the following Internet links and form an opinion as to what kinds of activities should and shouldn't be allowed, including hunting and whale watching.

1. Why is the Bowhead whale considered an endangered species?

2. What are some of the reasons for the declining Bowhead whale population?

3. Do you think that aboriginal whale hunting is the sole source of the declining Bowhead population?

4. What can people do to protect the Arctic Ocean environment and through this, the Bowhead whales?

5. How might whale watching be harmful to the whale population?

6. How might whale watching be helpful to the whale?

Internet Links

♦ Whale Watching in the Arctic at http://www.ngo.grida.no/ngo/wwfap/whalewatching/erich_hoyt.shtml

♦ Bowhead Whale—Historical and Current Status at http://nmml.afsc.noaa.gov/CetaceanAssessment/bowhead/bmsos.htm

  • What other information do you think is important to the Environmental Protection Agent point-of-view on this topic? Why do you think so?

  • Click here if you would like to use a template (available at http://rhem.spschools.org/specialprojects/webquest/animaltemplate.html) to help you in organizing your multimedia presentation.

Conclusion

Now that you've worked through activities in your role, you can see that the issues are much more complex than they first appear. View each other's presentations and then discuss the issues. Is your class able to come to a consensus on the original question: Should *all* hunting of Bowhead whales be prohibited? How do you think this might relate to this issue in real life? Did your view change from the beginning of the WebQuest?

Real World Action

Now it's time to put your learning into some real world activities. Choose one or more of the following ideas to follow up on your learning:

1. Write a letter to your local newspaper or your government outlining your views on the topic of Bowhead whale hunting. Give reasons for your opinion. Ask permission from your teacher and your parents before you mail or e-mail it to the newspaper. Be sure to proofread it.

2. Write or e-mail a letter to students in an Arctic school. Communities may have been involved in recent hunts, and students there might have a unique perspective on these issues. Click here (http://rhem.spschools.org/specialprojects/webquest/letter.html) to find some guidelines for writing your letter.

3. Visit the Whale and Dolphin Conservation Society homepage (http://www.wdcs.org/). Consider whether you and your classmates might want to adopt a whale to help with the education and conservation of these creatures.

4. Join your local "Walk for Whales and Dolphins." Check the Whale and Dolphin Society Walk page (http://www.wdcs.org/) to see if there is one in your area.

Evaluation

After groups have been introduced to the topic, have some background information, and understand the task, have them view the following assessment rubrics to guide their work.

♦ Teacher assessment rubric—Multimedia Project (http://rhem.spschools.org/specialprojects/webquest/teacherrubric.html)

♦ Student assessment rubric—Group Work (http://rhem.spschools.org/specialprojects/webquest/studentrubric.html)

After the conclusion of the WebQuest, have the student assess their own work in their group, as well as discuss your evaluation of their multimedia presentation. Feel free to modify these rubrics to suit your own group and grade level.

Using a WebQuest

The tasks in a WebQuest can be used as is or adapted depending on your learning goals and the grade level of the learners. The benefit of having the links embedded means that students can focus on the tasks at hand, rather than spending precious computer time doing ineffective or time-consuming searches. WebQuests often include rubrics and checklists that correspond with the learning outcomes chosen by the teacher-author, which is an added benefit.

Technology Connection

If you are trying a WebQuest with young learners or students who have difficulty reading, try using a text-to-speech tool to help them understand the content of the linked pages. Macintosh Operating System X has a built-in text-to-speech tool, and others are free or very inexpensive downloads (e.g., Universal Reader available at http://www.premier-programming.com/UR/Ureader.htm or Read Please available at http://readplease.com, both for Windows).

Tying Things Together

Chapter 3 described some of the lesson structures that can help to support teachers in differentiating by interest. Using lesson structures that provide interest choices can increase student engagement, but they must be designed with specific learning outcomes in mind.

For Further Reflection

1. How are the activity structures described in this chapter similar and different to my current practices?

2. How can I use or adapt these ideas to support differentiation?

3. How could I collaborate with colleagues to create lessons that are differentiated by interest?

4

Lesson Plans

Benevolence alone will not make a teacher, nor will learning alone do it. The gift of teaching is a peculiar talent, and implies a need and a craving in the teacher himself.

—John Jay Chapman

This chapter includes a variety of lessons in several subject areas that are differentiated by interest. Many of the current books on differentiation tend to avoid this, and for valid reasons. The core of differentiation is in knowing your students, and using someone else's lesson *as is* may not meet the needs of a particular group of learners or the specific outcomes from local curriculum. An important part of learning to differentiate, however, is in studying examples. This helps to give teachers a picture of what differentiation could look like. From there, adaptation and experimentation can occur.

It must be emphasized, however, that before a teacher differentiates, it is very important to understand the learners first, and then to differentiate based on observed needs and prescribed standards. In this way, a teacher would likely not use these lessons as they are, but would make adaptations according to what their students need. Chapter 5 provides information and step-by-step plans describing how to create a lesson or adapt an existing lesson. Study these lessons with a critical eye, and consider how they might be adapted for each unique group of learners.

Language Arts:
Multiple Intelligences Book Report: Tic-Tac-Toe

Learning Goals

Students will:

> **Know:** How to relate the important events and characters in of a story of choice.
>
> **Understand:** Books have important events and characters.
>
> **Do:** Describe the events and characters of a chosen book (Figure 4.1).

Figure 4.1. Tic-Tac-Toe Book Report

Verbal/Linguistic	Logical/Mathematical	Visual/Spatial
Create a poem about the events of the story or a main character.	Create a timeline that describes the important events of the story.	Draw or paint your favorite character. Around the artwork, add words that explain what you think is special or important about the character.
Musical/Rhythmic	**Free Choice**	**Intrapersonal**
Write a rap or song that tells about one or more events in your story. You can choose to perform it live or video or audio tape it.	Create an activity of your choice. Check with your teacher before you begin.	Imagine that you are the main character in your story. Create a series of diary entries (either written or tape recorded) that tell about some of the main events and how you feel about them.
Interpersonal	**Naturalist**	**Body/Kinesthetic**
With one or two classmates, create a commercial to promote your book. Be sure to share about the events and characters that would entice others to read the book.	Using recycled objects, create a three-dimensional scene from your book. Tell about why the scene is important in the development of the story (orally or in writing).	Create a dramatization of one or two scenes from your book. Tell why you chose the scenes and how they are important in the story.

Language Arts:
Reading Comprehension: Cubing

Learning Goals

Students will:

Know: How to relate the five Ws (+ how) from a reading passage.

Understand: Texts convey a message that can help to answer the reader's questions.

Do: Describe the five Ws (+ how) from a reading passage.

Suggested Activities

- This cube can be used for any subject or level where reading comprehension is required in both fiction and nonfiction texts.
- Students could roll the die individually and then respond to the question that lands face up. Sharing could take place in a small group or as a whole class.
- Seat students in a circle and give them a cube to roll after reading a story or other text. Students take turns rolling the die and providing an answer to the question that lands face up on the die (see Figure 4.2).

Figure 4.2. Five Ws + How Cube

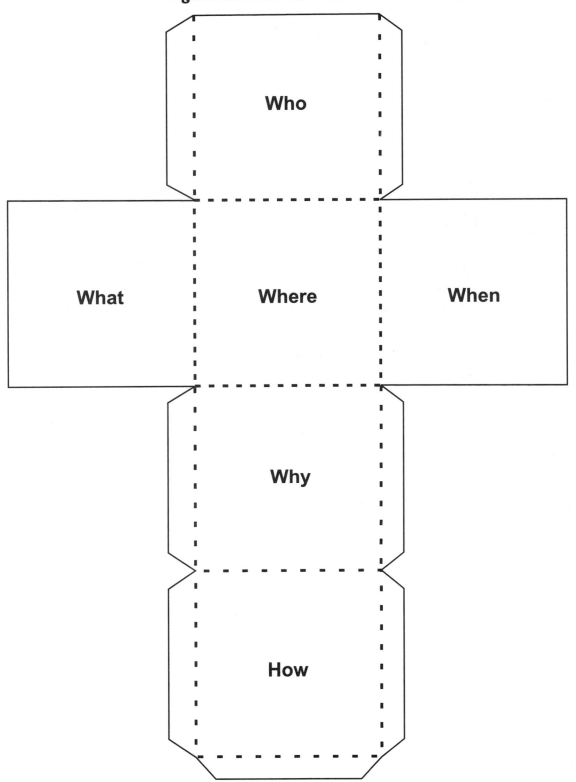

Language Arts:
Poetry: Learning Contract

Learning Goals

By completing the activities in this learning contract, you will

Know:

+ The structure of different types of poetry
+ How to create different types of poetry
+ How to read poetry in a way that conveys the meaning of the poem effectively

Understand:

+ That poetry can communicate an idea in a way that makes an impact
+ That poetry can be used to create a mood, feeling, or character

Do: Experiment with various forms of poetry by creating and/reading various types.

Choose Three of the Following Activities

Activity 1

Read through books, Internet sites, magazines, and so forth. Find a poem that creates a particular mood. Choose a piece of music that suits the mood of the poem and practice reading the poem to the music.

Activity 2

Create a poem that has a rhyming pattern. Identify the pattern you used and tell why you chose it. Explain how the rhyming pattern contributes to the mood of the poem.

Activity 3

With a partner, find a poem that can be read by two distinct voices. Create the voices and practice reading the poem with your partner.

Activity 4

Create a poem of any type that creates a mood. Practice reading it to others and have them guess the intended mood. Revise the poem based on their comments.

Activity 5

Read through books, Internet sites, magazines, and so forth. Find a poem that creates a strong character. Based on the poem, draw a picture of the character. Be able to tell about why the character is strong.

Culmination Suggestion

Hold a *Poetry Café* where students read original poems or the poetry of others. Use soft lighting and create the illusion of a cozy café. Consider inviting parents or other students to celebrate the students' learning. The audience snaps their fingers, rather than applauds after each poem.

Activities Chosen

_____ , _____ , _____

My activities will be complete and handed and/or ready to present by

_____

Student signature: _____

Teacher signature: _____

Parent signature: _____

Language Arts:

What a Character!: Role, Audience, Format, and Topic Project (RAFT)

Learning Goals

Students will:

Know: What story characters are and what makes them unique.

Understand: Different characters have different qualities and each contribute to the development of a story.

Do: Choose a role to creatively demonstrate an understanding of story characters (see Figure 4. 3).

Figure 4.3. Character RAFT

Role	Audience	Format	Topic
Psychiatrist	Hospital	Patient chart	This character has more than a few problems!
Actor	Movie Studio	Plea	Why using my character would make a great movie
TV Reporter	TV Audience	Interview/ Feature report	News at 6:00. This character is unique!
Student	Story character	Thank you note	The many reasons why you helped to make the story so memorable
Story Character	Newspaper Readers	Advice column	How you can avoid making the same mistakes that I did…
Story Character	Potential Readers	Song, rap or poem	A convincing way to describe many ways I'm special

Language Arts:
Spelling: Cubing

Learning Goals

Students will:

Know: The spelling patterns.

Understand: Spelling patterns can be used to spell unfamiliar words.

Do: Generalize the pattern of by applying it to the correct spelling of new words.

Note: The spelling cubes could be used with any word list from any spelling program that uses patterns to reinforce correct spelling (see Figure 4.4).

As a Class

Review the spelling pattern(s) for the week. Have students brainstorm words that fit the pattern(s).

Individually

Students roll the word study cube and the meaning cube (Figure 4.5) to determine the task(s) they will do with the words they will study for the week.

Figure 4.4. Word Study Cube

Divide each word into syllables.

Draw lines around the shape of each word.

Find as many rhyming words as possible for your words.

Write a sentence telling about any patterns you can find in your words.

Write your words in alphabetical order.

Create rainbow writing by tracing over your words with at least 3 different colors of felts or crayons.

Figure 4.5. Meaning Cube

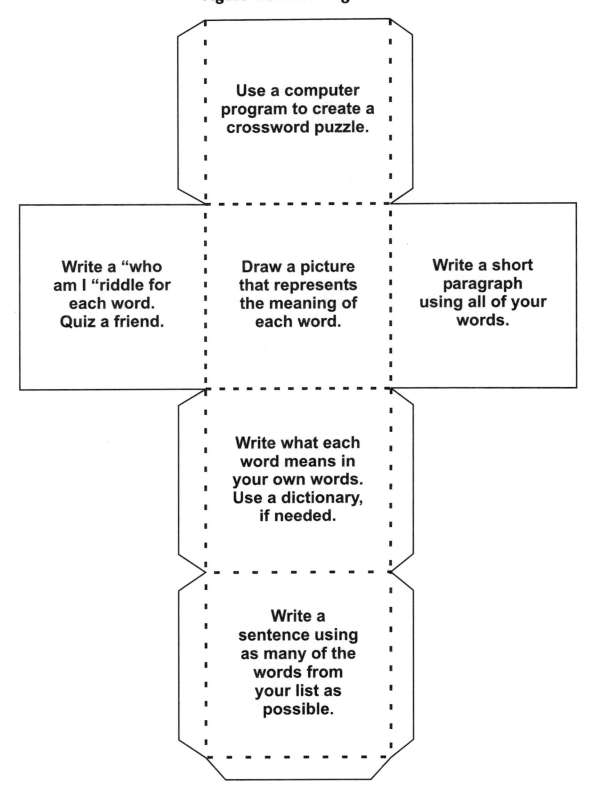

Language Arts:
Vocabulary: Choice Board

Learning Goals

Students will:

Know: The meanings of key words in language arts (or other subject areas).

Understand: Key terms that can help us understand text and communicate ideas.

Do: Identify key vocabulary words and choose a method to help remember the words. Consider using high frequency words and vocabulary crucial for understanding subject area content.

Hook

Play a word game such as Scrabble or Boggle, or introduce online word-play sites.

Activity

Teacher presents and models the various vocabulary strategies for the class. Students use the choice board (Figure 4.6) to choose methods of remembering vocabulary words.

Figure 4.6. Choice Board

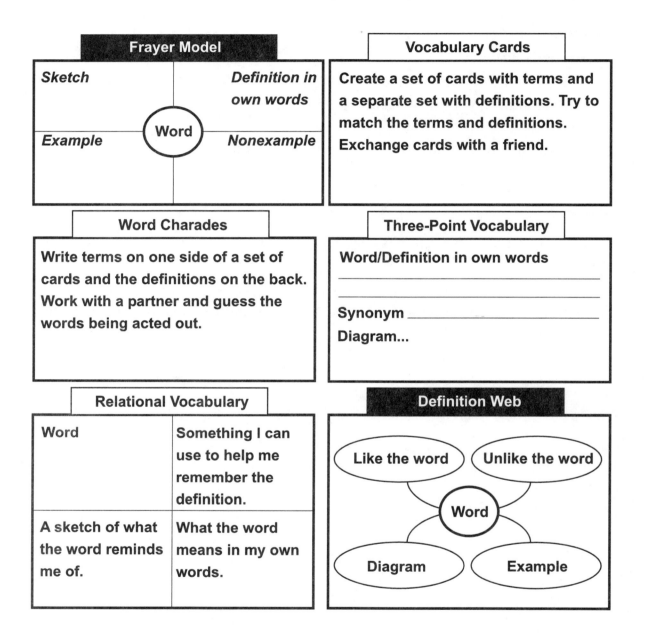

Math:

Fractions: Choice Board

Learning Goals

Students will:

Know: Fractions show parts of a whole and can be expressed numerically.

Understand: Fractions represent equal sized portions or *fair shares.*

Do: Use different materials to demonstrate what the fraction looks like.

Hook

Read *The Hershey's Milk Chocolate Fractions Book* by Jerry Pallotta.

Activity

Teacher gives students simple or more complex fractions to represent, depending on their level of readiness. Students should represent their fractions in as many ways as possible in the time frame given, choosing from the Pizza Choice Board (Figure 4.7).

Figure 4.7. Pizza Choice Board

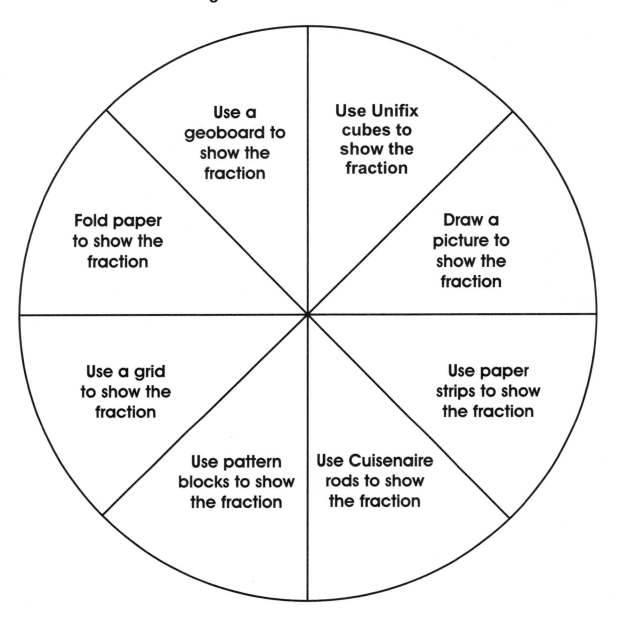

Math:

Math in Everyday Life: Learning Contract

By Completing the Activities in This Learning Contract, You Will

Know: Math is an important part of everyday life.

Understand: People use math every day to solve real-world problems.

Do: Explore ways math is used in everyday life.

Hook

Play a computer simulated game such as Lemonade Stand, Hot Dog Stand, or Roller Coaster Tycoon as an example of how math is used in everyday life.

Process Choices

You may work alone, with a partner or in a small group.

Core Activities (Choose One)

Core Activity 1

Find a person who uses fractions in his or her everyday life. Explain how they use them and create an example of how they use math to solve problems.

Core Activity 2

Research a career that requires a math background. Explain why math is an important part of their job.

Core Activity 3

Think of how you use math in everyday life. Create and explain examples.

Enrichment Activities

♦ Choose **one** if you work alone or with a partner, choose **two** if working in a small group.

Enrichment Activity 1

Create a song or rap that describes why math is important in everyday life.

Enrichment Activity 2

Create a storybook where the message of the story is about the importance of math.

Enrichment Activity 3

Create a PowerPoint presentation, Web Page, or Wiki (a Web site or similar online resource that allows users to add and edit ideas collectively) about why math is important in everyday life.

Enrichment Activity 4

Create a board game that illustrates how math is important in everyday life.

Enrichment Activity 5

Create a mural or bulletin board display that shows how math is important in everyday life.

Enrichment Activity 6

Create a play or video that shows how math is important in everyday life.

Enrichment 7

Write a love letter to "math" that shows your affection for it in how it helps you every day.

Enrichment Activity 8

Create a scrapbook using newspaper and magazine clippings that shows the importance of math in everyday life.

Activities Chosen

Core activity _____

Enrichment activities

_____, _____, _____

I choose to work (circle one):
alone   with a partner   in a small group

My activities will be complete and handed in by _____

Student signature: _____

Teacher signature: _____

Parent signature: _____

Math:

Geometric Solids: Cubing

Learning Goals

Students will:

Know: Characteristics of various geometric solids

Understand: Three-dimensional solids have particular characteristics and relationships and can be used to solve problems.

Do: Build, represent, and describe geometric solids

Hook

Go on a shape walk and look for geometric solids in the environment or read

Activity

1. Students roll task cube to determine their task.
2. Students roll either cube 1 or cube 2 to determine the shape they wil investigate.

Closure

Students share the products they create at *shape centers* where products from alike shapes can be shared (Figures 4.8, 4.9, 4.10). As other students view the projects, they investigate the shapes by filling in the Be a Shape Detective (Figure 4.11) sheet. Teacher reviews the characteristics of each geometric solid whereas student check for the accuracy of their findings.

Note: Cube 1 has simple geometric solids, while those on Cube 2 are more complex. The teacher could use one or the other, or both, depending on the needs of the students.

Figure 4.8. Task Cube

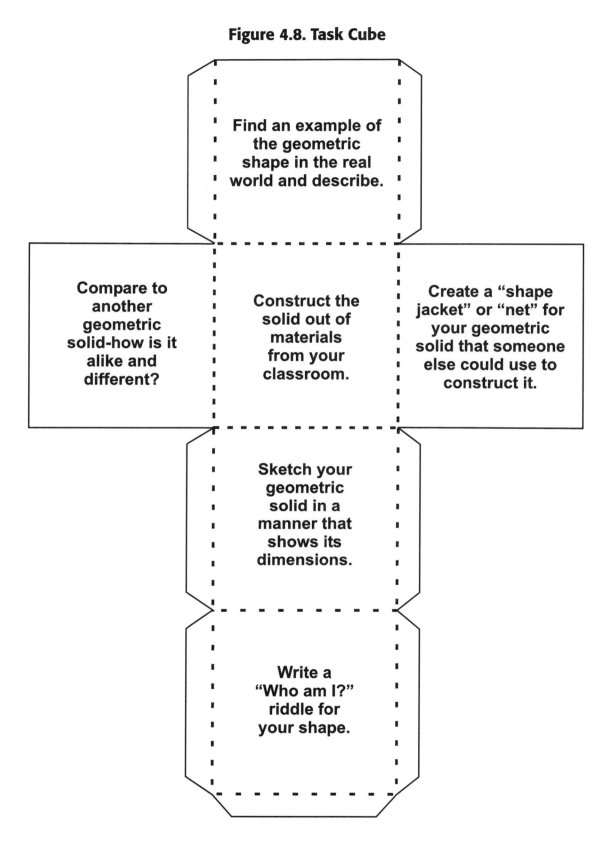

Find an example of the geometric shape in the real world and describe.

Compare to another geometric solid-how is it alike and different?

Construct the solid out of materials from your classroom.

Create a "shape jacket" or "net" for your geometric solid that someone else could use to construct it.

Sketch your geometric solid in a manner that shows its dimensions.

Write a "Who am I?" riddle for your shape.

Figure 4.9. Cube 1

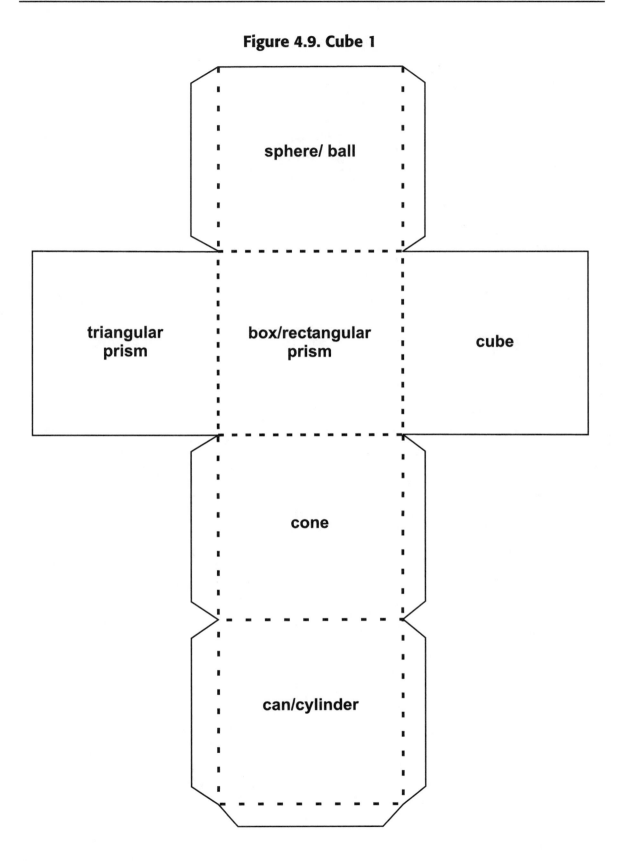

Figure 4.10. Cube 2

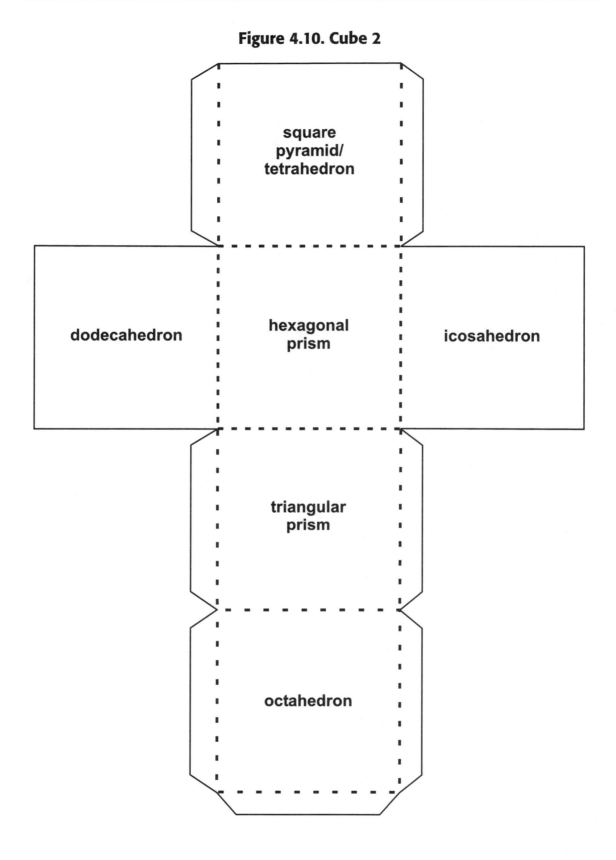

Be a Shape Detective!

Name _____

Investigate the shape projects that have been created and find out as much as you can about each shape.

Name of shape	Shape of each face	Number of faces	Number of edges	Number of vertices	Does it roll?	Does it slide?

Math:

Graphing: Cubing

Learning Goals

Students will:

Know: How to collect and display data in a variety of graphs to solve a problem (Figure 4.12).

Understand: Graphs can be used as a way to display and interpret data.

Do: Use different types of graphs to find information about a survey question.

Hook

Read *Who's Got Spots (Math Matters)* by Linda Aber

Activities

1. As a class, in small groups or as individuals, students create a survey question with which they can survey other students in the school and collect data.
2. The cube is rolled to determine how they will represent their data.
3. Students collect data through their survey question(s) and display the data in graph form.
4. Students use the data to answer the question and to make conclusions based on the results.

Closure

Students work in small groups or share with the whole class to compare their answers and discuss how the data they collected and displayed answered the question.

Figure 4.12. Graphs

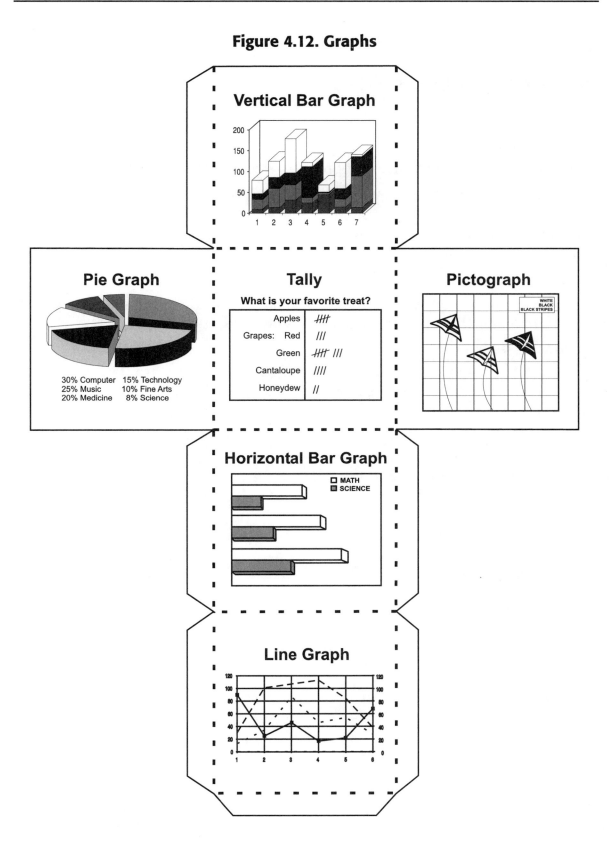

Math:

Patterning: Choice Board

Learning Goals

Students will:

Know: How to identify, name, reproduce, extend, and compare patterns.

Understand: Patterns can be found all around us and can be used to solve problems.

Do: Use various ways to identify, name, reproduce, extend and compare patterns.

Hook

Go on a pattern walk around the school and/or outside. Have students work in partners or teams to find patterns and then share and discuss as a class.

Activities

Choose one or more patterning activities from the choice board (Figure 4.13). For each choice, name the pattern created (e.g., ABAB, AABBAABB, etc.)

Closure

Students share their patterns in small groups and see if others can identify their patterns. As a group, they compare the patterns to each other. As an extension, extend one or more patterns and the *author* of the pattern checks to see if they were successful.

Figure 4.13 Patterning Choice Board

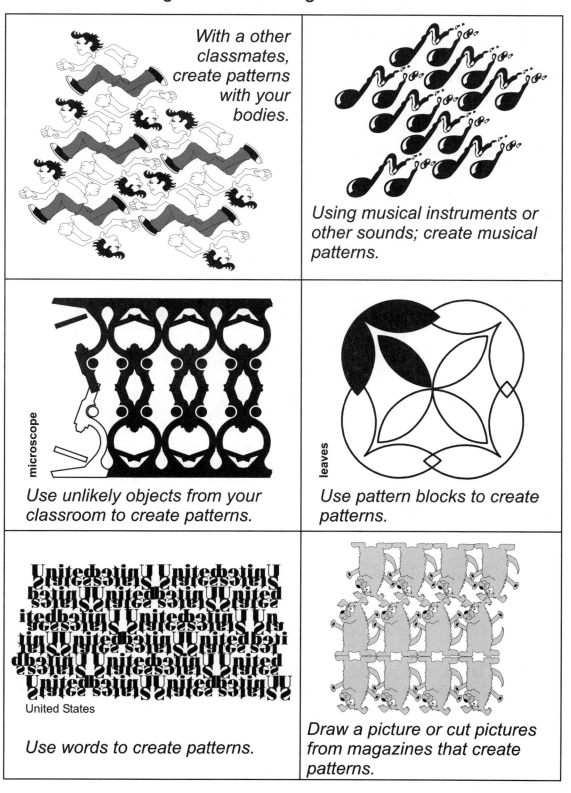

With a other classmates, create patterns with your bodies.

Using musical instruments or other sounds; create musical patterns.

microscope

Use unlikely objects from your classroom to create patterns.

leaves

Use pattern blocks to create patterns.

United States

Use words to create patterns.

Draw a picture or cut pictures from magazines that create patterns.

Science:

Life Cycles of Insects: RAFT

Learning Goals

Students will:

Know: How to explain and identify the life stages of an insect (Figure 4.14).

Understand: Insects go through predictable stages in life that repeat over and over.

Do: Describe and demonstrate an understanding of the life cycle of a particular insect.

Figure 4.14. Insect Life Cycle RAFT

Role	Audience	Format	Topic
Egg	Adults	Poem	I've got potentiality!
Larva	Other larva	Play	I don't want to grow up!
Adult	Larva	Chart	I'm tired of all this responsibility!
Pupa	Adults	Song or rap	Please release me, let me go!

Closure

Students share their projects in groups with at least one of each of the roles present in the group and compare the similarities and differences in each stage using a Venn diagram or other graphic organizer.

Science:

Understanding Plants: Cubing

Learning Goals

Students will:

Know: The names and functions of plant parts.

Understand: Plants have different parts that all play a role in keeping the plant alive and healthy.

Do: Create a product that demonstrates an understanding of plant parts (Figure 4.15).

Figure 4.15. Plant Cube

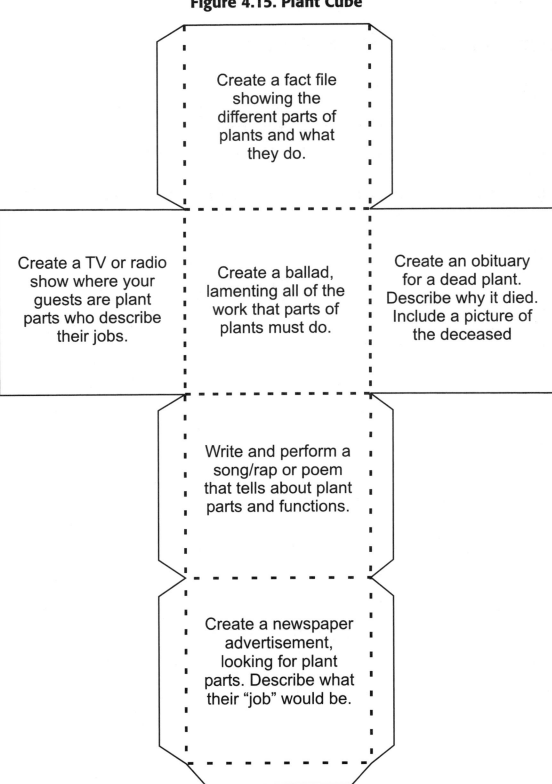

Science:

Fossils: RAFT

Learning Goals

Students will:

Know: Different types of fossils and how they are formed.

Understand: Fossils show conditions have changed over time.

Do: Demonstrate an understanding of fossils by creating a project to teach younger students (Figure 4.16).

Hook

Examine real-life fossils and/or create plaster-of-paris fossils.

Figure 4.16. Fossil RAFT

Role	Mother Nature
Audience	Younger students
Format	Skit, children's book, cartoon, chart, song, rap or student (negotiated with the teacher) choice
Topic	Teach younger students about fossils (what they are, how they are formed, different types, why they are important to study)

Closure

Visit a class of younger students so that the projects can be shared. Discuss whether the students feel their projects were successful in helping younger students understand fossils.

Science:

Changes in Matter: Cubing

Learning Goals

Students will:

Know: The states of matter (solid, liquid, gas).

Understand: States of matter change depending on the molecular motion in the matter.

Do: Through a variety of learning activities, demonstrate an understanding of the different states of matter and how they differ.

Learning Activities

Students roll cube 1 (Figure 4.17) to determine the type of matter they will investigate and then the activity cube (Figure 4.18) to determine how they will present their information.

Figure 4.17. Cube 1

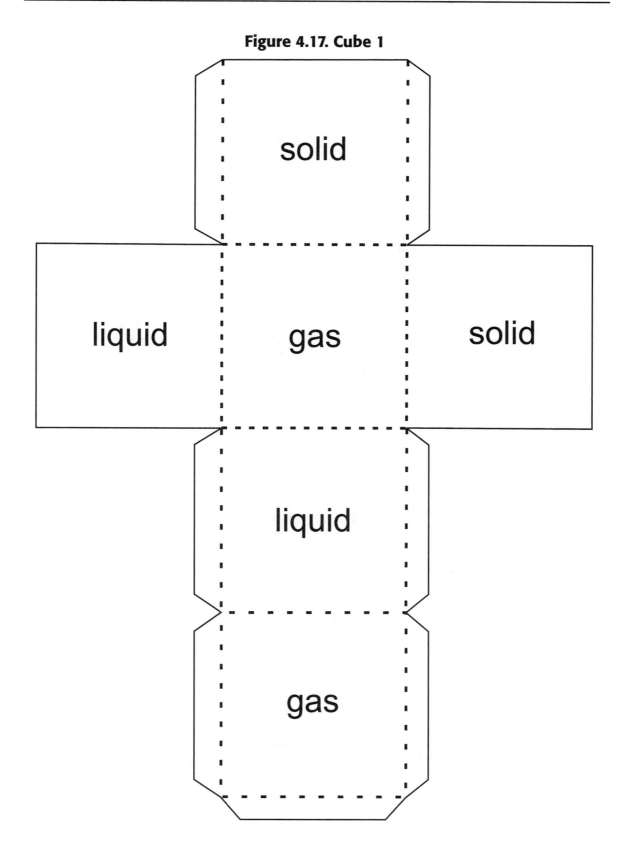

Figure 4.18. Activity Cube

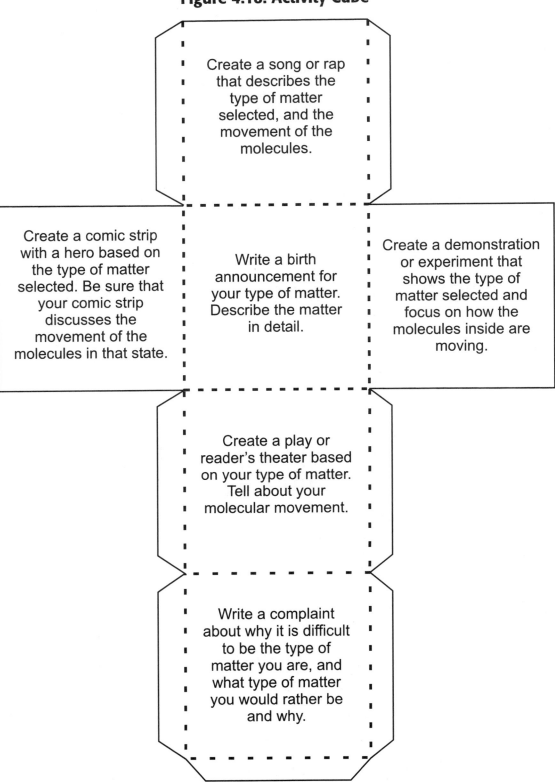

Science:

Managing Waste: Learning Contract

By Completing the Activities in This Learning Contract, You Will

Know:

♦ The kinds of waste that result from human activity.

♦ Ways in which materials can be reduced, reused, or recycled

Understand: That human activity can lead to the production of wastes, and identify alternatives for the responsible use and disposal of materials.

Be Able to **Do:**

♦ Identify alternative processes that can decrease the amount of waste produced

♦ Identify actions that individuals and groups can take to minimize the production of wastes and to recycle or reuse wastes

♦ Create ways to encourage others to reduce, reuse, and recycle their trash.

Choose One of the Following Core Activities

Activity 1

Create a graph or tally chart to represent the garbage your family produces at home over a period of three days that is not being recycled. Decide if any of the trash could be recycled or reused before going to the landfill. Write a note to your family with a description of how they could help the environment with their waste disposal.

Activity 2

Create a survey that asks students in your school about their family's recycling habits. Ask as many students as you are able to, and organize the information you collect. Report back to your classroom, and to other classrooms if you can, to describe what you found and what actions might be taken to improve the recycling habits in your community.

Activity 3

Create a diary from the point of view of a trash can. Write about what people throw away, and whether it really belongs in the trash, or if it could be reused or recycled.

Choose One of the Following Enrichment Activities

Enrichment activity 1

Create a song or a rap that encourages people to reduce, reuse, or recycle to preserve the environment.

Enrichment activity 2

Create a poster to encourage students to bring garbage-free lunches to school. Create the poster from recycled materials.

Enrichment Activity 3

Create an advertisement for TV (using video) or radio (using audio) that explains about the importance of reducing, reusing, and recycling trash.

Enrichment Activity 4

Create a catchy slogan and put it on bumper sticker that encourages people to recycle.

Activities Chosen

Core activities _____

Enrichment activity _____

My activities will be complete and handed in by _____

Student signature: _____

Teacher signature: _____

Parent signature: _____

Science:

Understanding Insects: Choice Board

Learning Goals

Students will:

Know: The characteristics of insects.

Understand: Insects have particular characteristics and parts and are different from other kinds of bugs.

Do: Create a product that demonstrates an understanding of characteristics that are particular to insects (Figure 4.19).

Figure 4.19. Insect Choice Board

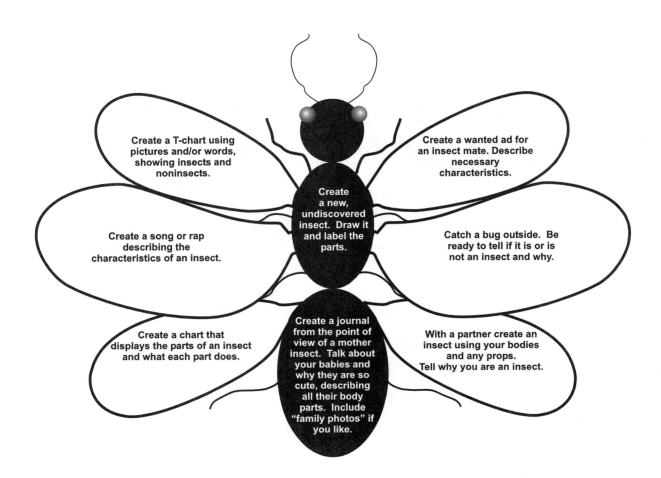

Social Studies:
My Family: Cubing

Learning Goals

Students will:

Know: That different kinds of family members have many responsibilities.

Understand: Family members each have a role, and rely on one another.

Do: Create a product that demonstrates an understanding of the different roles and responsibilities within a family (Figure 4.20).

Figure 4.20. Family Cube

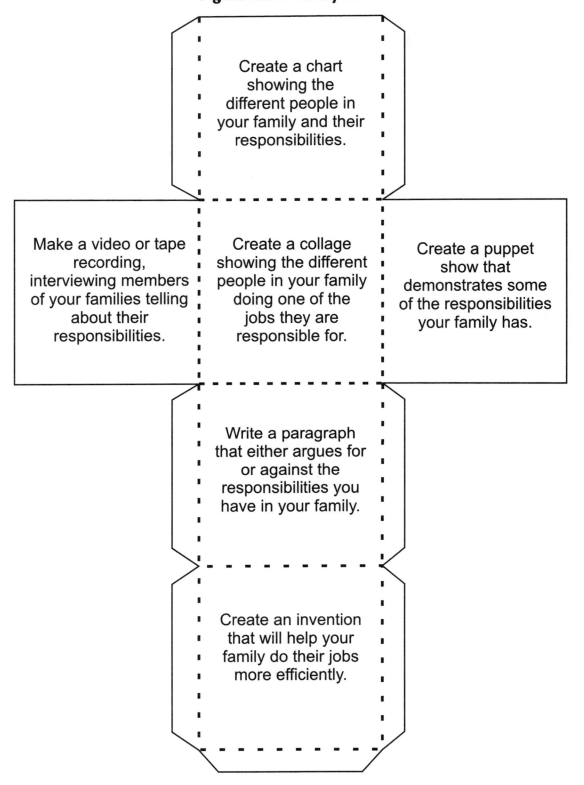

Social Studies:
My School: Tic-Tac-Toe

Learning Goals

Students will:

Know: The different people in the school that make up the school community.

Understand: The school community is made of many people who have different roles and responsibilities and that all roles are important.

Do: Demonstrate an understanding of one or more people involved in making up the school community.

Figure 4.21. My School Tic-Tac-Toe

Make a tape-recorded interview of someone in your school community. Be sure to have your questions ready before you start the interview.	Collect items from around the school that tell about different people in the school and what they do. Be able to share about what each item represents.	Spend some time following a person in the school to find out what they do. Share this information in a written or oral report.
Create a survey to determine which jobs students think are the most important in the school. Share the results orally or in writing.	Free space! Choose any role in the school and think of a way to show how they contribute to the school community.	Create a newspaper wanted advertisement for a job in the school. Be sure to tell job applicants what kinds of skills they need to do this job.
Create a pantomime of different people in the school that shows some of the jobs that they do.	Take digital pictures or make drawings of a person in your school and create a scrapbook that describes what they do.	Create a slogan for a bumper sticker that represents a role and responsibility in your school.

Social Studies:

Current Events
Learning Contract: Understanding Conflict

Learning Goals

Students will:

Know: Common elements of disputes and the challenges in resolving them.

Understand: Peaceful coexistence of people is an ongoing challenge in the world.

Do:

- ♦ Use an current event to understand the elements of a dispute and potential solutions.
- ♦ Demonstrate an understanding of the complexity of conflict.

Core Activities (choose one)

Choose a current event from the newspaper, a reputable news Web site or magazine that describes a conflict.

Within the core activity chosen, be sure to address the following key questions:

1. What are the causes of this conflict?
2. Who is involved?
3. What are the reasons the conflict been prolonged?
4. What would have to occur between the involved parties for the conflict to end?
5. How do you think this conflict could be resolved?
6. How could similar conflicts be avoided?

Core Activity 1

Create a mock press conference or newscast. In the content of your project, be sure to describe the five Ws (who, what, where, when, and why) of your story.

Core Activity 2

Create a Venn diagram where each circle describes the key points on both side of the conflict, and the middle describes what both sides might have in common or what they might be able to agree on in the future.

Core Activity 3

Write a letter to the editor of the publication. Tell about your understanding of the conflict and about your personal opinion.

Enrichment Activities (Choose 1):

Enrichment Activity 1

Create a song or a poem that describes conflict and how to resolve it peacefully.

Enrichment Activity 2

Create a poster or a play for younger students that could help them to resolve their conflicts peacefully.

Enrichment Activity 3

Create a manual that outlines the steps for effective conflict resolution.

Activities Chosen:

Core activity _____

Enrichment activity _____

My activities will be complete and handed in by _____

Student signature: _____

Teacher signature: _____

Parent signature: _____

Social Studies:
Mapping Skills: Choice Board

Learning Goals

Students will:

Know: Maps have different components and come in different forms.

Understand: Maps represent features or objects on the ground and can give people important information about their surroundings.

Do: Create a map to identify features of neighborhoods, cities, states and countries, and so on.

Task

Together, discuss why maps are important and what students know about them. Have students create a map (Figure 4.23), and choose the task based on standards and student readiness. Examples of places to map include the classroom, the playground, the school, the neighbourhood, the city/town, and so on. Depending on the grade level of students and the type of map, you can ask them to include some or all of the features in Figure 4.22.

Figure 4.22 Map Features

Title	Latitude	Poles
Legend	Longitude	Hemispheres
Symbols	Elevation	Equator
Compass rose	Location grid	Scale

4.23. Mapping Choice Board

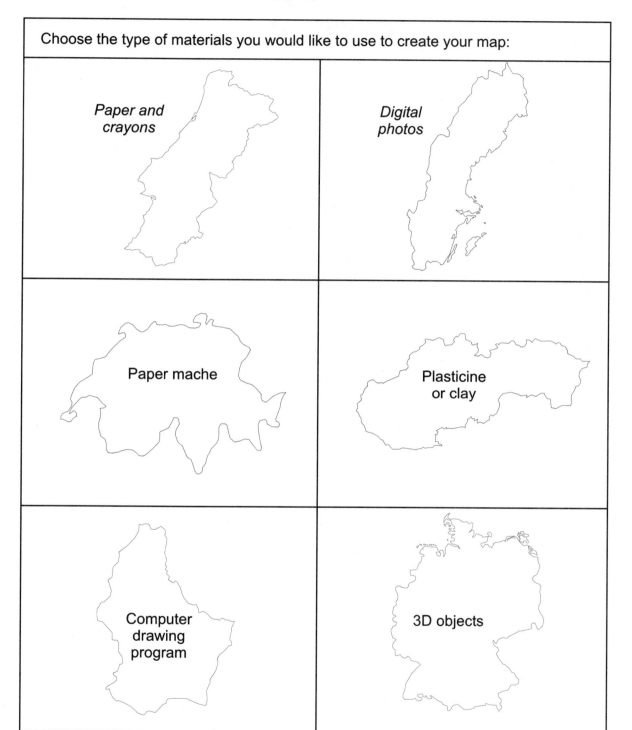

Choose the type of materials you would like to use to create your map:

Paper and crayons

Digital photos

Paper mache

Plasticine or clay

Computer drawing program

3D objects

Social Studies:

Rights and Responsibilities: Cubing

Learning Goals

Students will:

> **Know:** People have both rights and responsibilities in society.
>
> **Understand:** The differences between having rights and responsibilities and how understanding these concepts can make good citizens.
>
> **Do:** Create a product that demonstrates an understanding of rights and responsibilities.

Task

Roll the Rights and Responsibilities cube (Figure 4.24), Description cube (Figure 4.25), and the Product cube (Figure 4.26) to determine how understanding of the topic will be represented.

Figure 4.24. Rights and Responsibilities Cube

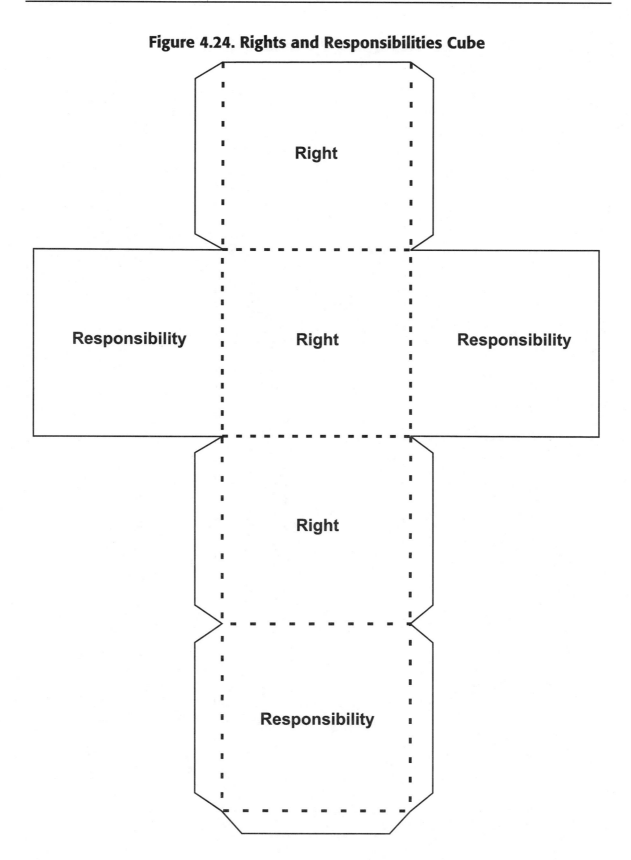

Figure 4.25. Description Cube

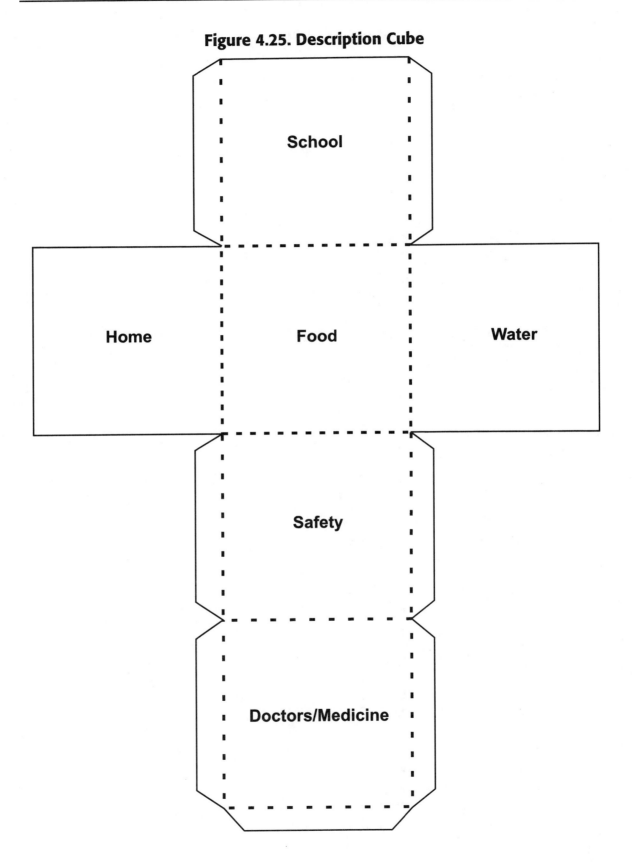

Figure 4.26. Product Cube

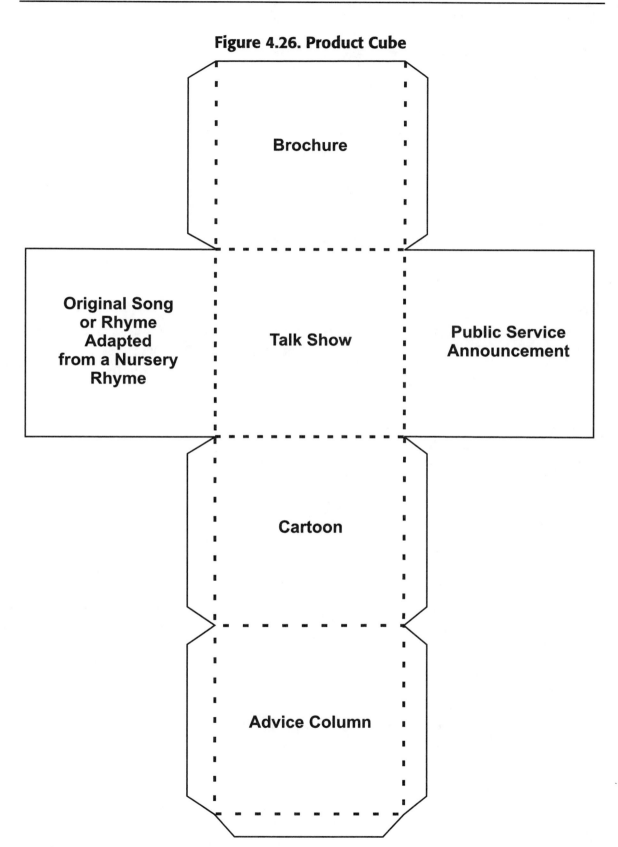

Social Studies:
Communities in the Present and Past: RAFT

Learning Goals

Students will:

Know: What characteristics define communities of the present and of the past; know what is unique about these communities.

Understand: How communities evolve from the past to the present and appreciate how the past and present are connected.

Do: Create a product that demonstrates an understanding of communities in the past and present (Figure 4.27).

Hook

View a selection of digital pictures of a community in the present and in the past. Have students work in teams to sort the pictures into past and present and have reasons why they placed them in each category. For an extra challenge, have them guess the year of each photo.

Figure 4.27. Communities Past and Present RAFT

Role	A child of your age in the past or in the present
Audience	A child of the opposite time period than you chose
Format	Diary entries, song, poem, magazine advertisement, play, or other idea (check with your teacher first)
Topic	Convince a child in the opposite time period that it would be better to live in the time period that you do.

Culmination

Students present their projects and do a think/pair/share about why we should understand and appreciate the past, and how it is connected to the present.

Social Studies:
Historical Events Timeline: Choice Board

Learning Goals

Students will:

Know: The sequence of key historical events.

Understand: That examining the sequence can help us to understand the causes and effects of historical events.

Do: Choose a method to construct various time lines of key events, people, and periods of the historical era of study.

Figure 4.28. Historical Events Choice Board

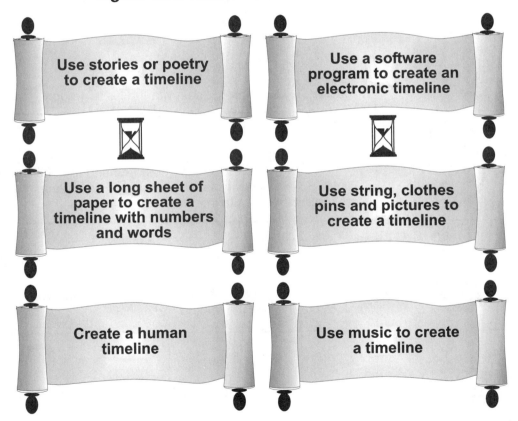

Closure

Share various timelines and discuss what information was gathered from each type of timeline and how it helps us to understand the historical event.

Learning Contract: Group Work

Figure 4.29. Group Roles

	Materials	Collects materials to do task, holds chart paper for reporter, posts products on walls.
	Recorder	Writes group ideas.
	Reporter	Shares ideas with the large group.
	Timekeeper	Notes the start time and end time for the activity. Gives the groups prompts at five minute intervals.
	Task Master	Keeps group on topic and on task with gentle reminders.
	Hitchhiker	Gathers ideas from other groups and brings back to help with the group task.
	Encouragers	Encourages all group members to participate and provides positive feedback on contributions.

Group Work Learning Contract

Group members: _____

_____

Group task: _____

Group responsibilities: _____

_____

Our project will be complete by _____

Group Roles:

Materials will be handled by _____

Recording will be done by _____

Reporting to the class will be done by _____

Time for our task will be kept by _____

The task master for our task will be _____

The hitchhiker for our task will be _____

The encourager(s) for our project will be _____

We agree that we will perform our individual duties and work as a whole to keep the group working together well. If we have problems, we agree to try to resolve them together first and then ask for help if necessary.

Student signatures:

Teacher signature: _____

Date: _____

Tying Things Together

This chapter provides an array of lessons presented in various lesson structures, and in different subject areas. They are differentiated by interest and provide students choices in products and presentations. These lessons can be adapted for the unique needs of a classroom or can be used as a springboard to create new lessons. Chapter 5 will provide ideas about how these adaptations and new lessons can be created.

For Further Reflection

1. In what way could these lessons help to spark student interest and increase engagement?

2. How might I need to adapt these lessons to suit the needs of my learners?

3. What personal learning experiences have I had where being given choices helped to increase my motivation and understanding?

5

Creating a Lesson
and Adapting Lessons

It is the supreme art of the teacher to awaken joy in creative expression and knowledge.

—Albert Einstein

Chapter 4 gives specific lesson ideas for how to differentiate by interest for students. The real art in differentiating is when a teacher is able to accurately assess a particular group of students and then adjust lessons accordingly. In this way, the lessons presented in the previous chapter may or may not fit your learners, but Chapter 5 will outline how you can create new lessons or adapt existing ones.

Don't Bother Differentiating Fluff

When you first begin to plan for differentiation, there's no doubt that it takes some planning time up front. The one thing teachers probably do not want to do is to spend a great deal of time planning to differentiate a lesson that isn't an important understanding in a unit of study. If you are going to spend time planning to differentiate by interest, be sure that it is an outcome that is one of the key understandings that students must take time to internalize.

Checklist for Creating a Lesson Differentiated by Interest

The following checklist can be used when creating a lesson that is differentiated by interest. A reproducible copy of the checklist can be found on Blackline Master 23.

- ❑ Identify the subject and topic of study.
- ❑ Specify the outcomes (i.e., what the students should know, understand, and be able to do as a result of completing the activity). These should come from curriculum and standards documents.
- ❑ Decide on an activity structure that will allow students to choose a task that interests them (e.g., tic-tac-toe or other choice board; role, audience, format, and topic project [RAFT]; cubing; learning contract; WebQuest).
- ❑ Brainstorm activities that could possibly meet the learning outcomes.
- ❑ Eliminate the activities that will not lead the students to know, understand, and be able to do the important learning outcomes.
- ❑ Choose the activities that are the most engaging and will lead the students to the same learning outcomes.
- ❑ Describe the learning activities in detail. Create student handouts, if appropriate.

❑ Decide which parts of the activity will be assessed and how they will be assessed.

❑ Determine how you will bring closure to the activities and/or how you will facilitate the sharing of learning.

Lesson Plan Template

Using a template can be helpful when organizing a new lesson that is differentiated by interest (Figure 5.1). A blank lesson plan template can be found on Blackline Master 24.

Figure 5.1. Differentiating by Interest: Lesson Plan Template

Subject:	Topic:
Outcomes: As a result of this study, students should: **Know:** **Understand:** **Be able to do:**	
Lesson Structure: ❑ Choice board ❑ RAFT ❑ WebQuest	❑ Learning contract ❑ Cubing ❑ Other
Description of learning activities:	
Assessment:	
Closure/Sharing:	

Adapting Lessons

The benefit of a book, such as this one, is that it shows lesson examples so teachers have an idea of what differentiation might look like in the classroom. After that, teachers can take the ideas and then adapt them to their specific student needs.

The first thing on which the teacher must be clear, is who their students are and where they are at in terms of readiness, interest, and learning profile. Once this is established, the teacher can critically look at lessons and decide if they can be used "as is," or if they need to be adapted. A teacher may need to adapt them in some of the following ways:

- The text may need to be enlarged/made more explicit for younger learners or made more complex for older or more advanced learners.
- The number of task choices may need to be increased or reduced.
- The complexity of the tasks may need to be increased or reduced.
- The time required to complete the task may need to be adjusted.
- The evaluation criteria may need to be adjusted.
- The process of the tasks, including grouping or working individually may need to be adjusted.
- Choices may need to be added or removed to reflect the interests of a particular group of learners.

It is also helpful to study lesson examples as a collaborative school team. The more examples teachers have to look through, the more ideas they are able to generate themselves.

Product Choice Ideas

Whether creating lessons from scratch or adapting an existing one, it can be helpful to scan through a list of products that can be used for interest choices. A list of some potential interest choices follows (Figure 5.2).

Figure 5.2. Interest Project Ideas

Birth announcement	Web boards	Last will and testament
Puzzle	Wikis	Blueprints
Bumper sticker	Debate	Children's book
Change words to familiar songs	E-mail	Dialogues
Recipe	Timeline	Venn diagram
Classified ad	Love letter	WebQuests
Blogs	Storytelling	Experiment
Comic book	Talk show	PowerPoint
Audiotape	Database	Costumes
Dance	Fairy tale	Brochure
Slogan	Interview	Editorial
Diary/Journal	Petition	Riddles
Bulletin-board display	Puppet show	Code creation/Cracking
Drama	Speech	Web page
Eulogy	Review	Skit
Flyer	Graph	Project cube
Full page newspaper ad	Reenactment	Warning
Invention	Mind map	Sketch book
Jingle	Jokes	Melody
Kidspiration/Inspiration	Job description	Chart
Podcast	Wanted poster	Poem
Mock trial	Animation	Biography
Videotape/Digital video	Outdoor games	Comic strip
Obituary	Topic cube	Readers theatre
Online survey	Monologue	Magazine advertisement
Pantomime	Model	Role play
Personal history	Collections	Collage
Photo album	Survey	Personal ad
Picture dictionary	Press conference	Mural
Poster	Group discussion	Sculpture
Public service announcement	Recycled art	Newspaper
Rap	Map	Nursery rhyme
Scavenger hunt	Demonstration	Real-world problems
Scrapbook	Letter	Song
Sign	Announcement	Newscast
Spreadsheet	Game board	Fact file
Telecollaborative projects	Thank you note	Advice column
Travelogue	Complaint	Reflections
Stand-up comedy routine	Invitation	Photos/digital photos

Tying Things Together

This chapter provides strategies and ideas that can assist in adapting lessons that are differentiated by interest and how to create original lessons. Chapter 6 will uncover other issues including strategies for how teachers can assess in a differentiated classroom.

For Further Reflection

1. How will I determine when I am able to use an existing lesson and when I will need to adapt them?

2. With whom might I be able to collaborate to create new lessons?

3. How will I ensure that lessons used and created meet the needs of my learners as well as the important understandings that come from required curriculum and standards?

6

Assessment and Other Lingering Issues

Learning is not attained by chance, it must be sought for with ardor and attended to with diligence.

—Abigail Adams

As teachers begin to plan for differentiation, there are common issues that arise, such as how to assess, how to support gifted learners in the regular classroom, and how to bring closure to lessons where students are engaged in different learning activities. Chapter 6 provides strategies for these questions.

What is Assessment For?

Teachers are often concerned about how they will manage assessment where students are involved in multiple projects. They may ask questions like: How can I easily assess where students are at in their understanding? How will I assess when the products created are so different? Have I created an assessment nightmare? These are important questions, and must be thought through carefully. The first question that must be asked is about the nature of assessment. Why do we assess? There are two types of assessment that can be used—formative and summative—each plays a role in supporting student learning.

Formative Assessment
(Assessment "On the Fly")

Before we can adjust instruction, we must know where the students are. It is important to have a clear picture of their progress on an ongoing basis and not just at the end of a unit when it is too late to intervene if students do not understand the concepts. A key to differentiating involves knowing your students extremely well, so having easy to use, formative assessment strategies is extremely important. They help to provide a sense of where students are at so that you can decide if whole-group instruction will work, or if you will need to do some differentiating.

The following sections outline strategies and examples of some of these formative assessments.

Ticket in the Door

What Is It?

The teacher greets students at the door and hands them a piece of paper or index card (their "ticket"). A key question is posed on the white board, chalk board, or overhead (or, it could be photocopied on a slip of paper) that relates to the previous day's learning. It also can serve as a *sponge activity* as students get settled. The teacher would likely wish to do a quick partner share so that if all students didn't have an opportunity to do the activity, they would still to hear about their partner's ideas (and think about their own). See Figure 6.1.

Why Is It Effective?

It helps students activate their background knowledge and previous understanding. It helps the brain be ready to attach new learning to what is already known.

Figure 6.1. Ticket in the Door

Yesterday we learned about adjectives. List all the adjectives you can think of for the word "hot":

Exit Cards

What Are They?

The teacher poses one or more questions or phrases to which students respond at the end of a lesson. Students answer on a piece of paper or index card, sign their name, and deposit in a box or basket before they leave the classroom. See Figure 6.2.

Why Are They Effective?

Exit cards help students to think about what they understand to be the important learning from the class. It also enables the teacher to quickly find out which students understand a concept and who needs extra assistance. A sample of a 3-2-1 exit card can be found on Blackline Master 26.

Figure 6.2. Exit Card

3-2-1 Exit Card

3 key terms from our experiment today:

2 questions you have:

1 way you could apply what you have learned to another situation:

Thumbs Up

What Is It?

The teacher poses a key question or asks to gauge their comfort level with a concept. Students give a thumbs up if they are comfortable, thumbs to the side if they are neither comfortable nor uncomfortable, and thumbs down if they are confused or having difficulty.

Why Is It Effective?

It is a very quick check to see how many students are on target and how many are feeling lost. It can help for planning and for possible mini-lessons the next day. Having students put their heads down and closing their eyes before holding up their hands makes it less stressful for students if they are experiencing difficulties.

Portfolios

What Are They?

Portfolios are collections of student work that are designed to show growth over time. They can be organized in binders or file folders or other collection systems.

Why Are They Effective?

They are a great way to help students, parents, and teachers see the progress of a student. They can be used as a tool to help students become better at reflecting on their learning, progress, and goal setting. The teacher has students choose pieces of work for a particular reason (e.g., something to be proud of, something that was learned, something that shows growth). The reflection makes it an assessment tool as opposed to just a scrapbook or random collection of work. See Figure 6.3.

Figure 6.3. Portfolio Reflection

Date_____

I chose this piece to include in my portfolio because

When I did this piece, I learned

Something I would change for next time is

Give Me a Hand

What Is It?

The teacher poses a key question about a topic that will give him or her an idea of students' comfort level with a concept. Students raise the number of fingers that represents their comfort level with the topic (one being the least and five being the most).

Why Is It Effective?

It is a very quick check to see how many students are very comfortable and how many are a little lost. It can help for planning and for possible mini-lessons the next day. Having students put their heads down and closing their eyes before holding up their hands makes it less stressful for students if they are experiencing difficulties.

Anecdotal Notes

What Are They?

Although students work independently, the teacher circulates and writes down observable behaviors in which students are engaging.

Why Are They Effective?

It's a great way to be a bit of a *learner detective* and determine how students are progressing. They can become the basis for grouping and instruction in subsequent lessons. These notes can also be incorporated into report card comments.

Tips

Only choose a few (e.g., five or six) students to observe during one class period. Try using a file folder for each subject or class (if you teach in multiple classrooms) and tape index cards so they can be flipped up. Sticky notes can also work well. Write in different colors of pen for different concepts or activities and always date your observations. See Figure 6.4.

Figure 6.4. Anecdotal Notes Collection

Grade 5 Science	
Brock	Britt
Brayden	Jen
Jordan	Hailey
Chris	Alyssa
Matt	Madison
Steven	Jada
Jake	Amy
Ben	

Summative Assessment (Assessment at the End)

After a project or unit, we want to check student's learning as well have an opportunity to evaluate how they performed on their tasks.

Summative Assessment Considerations

◆ When students are creating multiple projects, it is possible to assess only one important component (the content, organization *or* conventions in writing, for example), or just choose one of their products at random to assess. Students might also be asked to choose one piece that they learned the most by doing, or one that they feel they did a good job with.

◆ Specific assessments can be created (see examples in the tiered assignment samples) or more generic-type rubrics can be used for many types of projects (See Blackline Master 27).

◆ Ensure that the assessment matches what students know, understand, and are able to do.

◆ Consider involving students in creating the assessment criteria for projects.

Must All Assignments Have an Assigned Grade?

Teachers often feel compelled to assign a grade to every piece of student work. Imagine if this were the case when you were learning how to drive. What if every mistake you make while you were learning to drive was held against you and counted toward your final assessment of whether you received your license or not? Although students are practicing and learning concepts, it can be preferable to give the students feedback orally or in writing and have the students complete a self-assessment so they can articulate where they are at and what they need to do next. This kind of feedback will help students to continue to learn. Giving grades for every task as they are learning may not fairly represent where they are because their learning along the way is averaged into a final grade.

Assessment in differentiated instruction is a whole topic of study in itself, and there are several books on assessment in differentiated instruction that would provide excellent follow up such as, *Fair Isn't Always Equal: Assessing & Grading in the Differentiated Classroom* by Rick Wormeli and *Differentiated Assessment Strategies: One Tool Doesn't Fit All* by Carolyn Chapman and Rita King. In addition, other books on assessment for learning are helpful when planning for differentiation. Consider books by Rick Stiggins, Robert Marzano, Art Costa, and Thomas Guskey.

Technology Connection

There are several sites that have previously created rubrics that teachers can access and adapt. A simple search with the word "rubric" and a project title or subject will reveal more rubrics that a teacher could use. Other online tools that I've used are online rubric generators, where you insert learning outcomes and descriptors into online forms, and you receive a polished, printable rubric when you are finished. One site that offers this type is Rubistar (http://rubistar.4teachers.org/index.php) . Ensure that the rubrics you use are aligned with required standards and outcomes.

Effective Self-Evaluation

Having students self-evaluate is another piece of the differentiated instruction assessment puzzle. Teachers are often dissatisfied with having students do self-evaluation because many tend to give vague responses that do not really show evidence of reflection. This can be partly because of student learning styles and a lack of clearly identified targets for success. Those who have a strong intrapersonal intelligence can find reflective activities quite easy, whereas others struggle given the task of being introspective.

The following is a process that can help students to become better self-assessors.

Steps for Teaching Effective Self-Evaluation

1. First, clearly explain the process for and reasons for doing self-evaluation to students. Better yet, do a think/pair/share and have the students tell you why it is important.

2. On an overhead, make a copy of the reflection sheet you want students to use, and model how you would complete it. Do a *write-aloud,* explaining the process you go through while thinking out loud about the project and choosing words to describe the project.

3. Together brainstorm a list of adjectives that could describe working through a process. Post this and leave it up all year.

4. Before having students complete a self-evaluation, give them some time to talk about their experiences with a partner or in a small group before they are expected to write.

5. Provide feedback and ask probing questions as they work through self-evaluations so they have an opportunity to improve.

6. Repeat this process as you use different types of reflective tools. Often, they need to see models and to practice before they become proficient self-evaluators.

Blackline Masters 28 through 32 provide examples of self-assessment and goal-setting tools.

Technology Connection

Blogging

Blogging is a form of Internet publishing that has grown enormously in popularity over the last few years. It is the common term for a "Web log," and it a chronological journal entry, most often used with readily available software. Blogs can be used to support independent studies for students who enjoy writing. They could set up a blog to create a brief description of their work each day. The software also allows for comments following each post, where the teacher could respond to the students' work and provide feedback or ask questions. Most blogging software is still free. Some of the most popular software used includes Blogger (http://www.blogger.com) and Blog (http://www.bblog. com).

The Mad Professor Factor

I remember one year early in my teaching career I had a student who was absolutely brilliant. He was able to solve very complex problems, do math and logic problems far beyond his years, and definitely needed some extra challenges in the regular classroom. I lovingly called him my "mad professor." I knew that he wasn't going to be engaged if I only gave him more of what he could already do, so using independent projects was going to be important in helping him to continue his learning. Early in the year, I set him off on his first independent project. I asked him what he would like to learn about, and he picked a topic. I sent him to the library to do research, and he never came back. I went to find out what happened to him, and he got lost in a book and forgot what his task was. The rest of the independent project was a little frustrating for both of us. He was interested in doing an independent study but lacked the organizational skills and structure to be able to complete a project on his own. That year, I learned a great deal about working with gifted students, many of whom are also "organizationally challenged." The following section outlines my hard-learned tips.

Hints for Using Independent Studies with Gifted Students in the Regular Classroom

- Assess their interest and special talents.
- Be aware of their needs (e.g., need for organization, help with writing, socialization).
- Give them a choice of a few topics that relate to what the class is studying. This will allow them to stay connected with their peers and to extend everyone's knowledge on the topic at hand. Leaving choices too open ended can make deciding on a project difficult.
- Using real-world problems is often a good choice for a project. In any case, the project needs to be engaging and authentic.
- Give directions in a written format that provides the "big picture" and then one step at a time.
- Clarify expectations and assessments before the project begins.
- Provide and encourage the use of a broad range of resources.
- Have frequent checkpoints so that if a student is encountering difficulty, the teacher can provide the necessary support.
- Provide an opportunity to share with the class, as well as any other audiences that make sense.

Checkpoints

Whether students are working on group or independent projects, it is important for them to keep track of what their goals are, what they accomplish, and what their next steps will be. This is not a skill that comes easily to many students, so they are important skills to teach.

There are several ways to accomplish this:

1. Have students mark important dates into their school reminder books (e.g., when drafts are due, when parts of a project are due, when the final product is due).

2. Create for students (or have them create) a timeline or checklist that outlines where they should be on their project on a given day.

3. Use a project log of some sort to help students determine where they are and where they will go during their next work time (See Figure 6.5 and Blackline Master 33—try making two per side and then double-side the pages to create a log book).

4. A series of steps that students could follow to create a project can be found on Blackline Master 34.

Figure 6.5. Project Log

What I worked on/completed:	What I still need to do:
I need:	Evaluation of my work time:

Closure

Whenever students are working on multiple projects, whether they are working individually or in groups, it's important to facilitate some sort of sharing. This allows students to learn from each others' experiences. The strategy chosen for sharing should be thought out in advance and should suit the products or ideas that the students create. This kind of closure helps to reinforce the idea that classrooms are a community of learning, where everyone has learned something slightly different but nevertheless important. The following strategies can be helpful in planning to bring closure to differentiated lessons.

Closure Strategies

Sharing Stations

Choose a few days when different students will share their work and limit this number to four or five students (or groups) per day. Situate the students in different parts of the classroom and then divide up remaining students into groups. Students share their project with the small group and the *audience* rotates through until all students have the opportunity to view each project. This process can take a bit more time, but it is much easier for students to focus and learn from each other. It also gives students more opportunities to tell about their project and gain confidence in speaking to groups. The audience also has more opportunity to view products up close and to ask questions.

Gallery Walks

Groups or individuals post their projects around the room. Students circulate in small groups to view the projects. The teacher can request that a *docent* remain at each project to answer questions the viewers have.

Web of Understanding

Students form a circle and face each other. The teacher starts by wrapping a length of yarn around his or her hand and states one thing he or she learned during the class or project. The teacher then tosses the yarn across the circle to another student who wraps length of yarn around his or her hand and states something he or she learned. The end result is a web, which can also represent the interconnectedness of learning in the classroom. The teacher may wish to close the sharing with a brief discussion of the interconnectedness of learning in the classroom.

Ball Toss Share

Similar to the Web of Understanding except a soft ball or beach ball is used.

Quiz Questions

Students create questions (and answers) that represent something they learned during the class or project. The teacher can use student questions as Tickets in the Door, Exit Cards, or as part of a short unit quiz.

Learning Quilt

Each student gets a square of paper. On the square the students can draw and/or write something that represents their most important learning. Tape or staple all the squares on a bulletin board together and create a learning quilt for a unit of study.

Tying Things Together

This chapter provides some ideas about some of the issues and questions that teachers can have as they begin to differentiate in their classrooms, such as assessment, how to help gifted learners in the regular classroom, and how to bring closure to a differentiated lesson. The Chapter 7 will provide guidance about how to get started in differentiating by interest and how to provide encouragement to continue down the road of differentiated instruction.

For Further Reflection

1. How do I bring closure to lessons in my classroom? How does it help to unite students as a learning community?
2. Where might I find additional resources and expertise in assessing in a differentiated classroom?
3. What are some of the goals you have in mind as you begin to differentiate?

7

Where to Start?

A journey of a thousand miles begins with a single step.

—Confucius

Because differentiated instruction is such a huge field of study, I wanted to focus this book on just one aspect of differentiating. Even so, just differentiating by interest can still seem a bit daunting. Here is my best advice for getting started:

- **Assess:** Start by discovering student interests, especially with the students who don't tend to share this information easily. It's not enough just to find out, however, we must also be prepared to use this information to engage students in their learning. Find some way to record this information so that it is in a system that is easy to retrieve and use.

- **Create a classroom environment that supports differentiation:** Teachers tend to do the getting-to-know-you activities at the beginning of the year but doing small things all year long helps to recognize and celebrate student interests and differences. Use literature to continually emphasize the importance of being unique.

- **Start planning using standards:** Begin planning with required standards. It will help to ensure that choices offered will help students understand the important concepts. Keeping them at the forefront of planning will also help to keep them as a focus when planning for assessment.

- **Start small:** Set a goal of trying at least one lesson that is differentiated by interest in the upcoming school year. Observe the response of your students and build on success. Try using the goal-setting sheet found on Blackline Master 35.

- **Don't reinvent the wheel:** To begin with, it might be easier to use an existing differentiated lesson or adapt a traditional lesson that is already written, rather than starting from scratch. With WebQuests, for example, there are hundreds of them on the World Wide Web. Make sure lessons fit your learning outcomes and then use or adapt. Once you have tried some lessons, it's much easier to create new ones, and eventually, it just becomes a part of how you think about planning.

- **Work together:** Much of my work when I began differentiating instruction was done with my job-sharing partner. It is much easier (and more fun) to generate ideas together. Many schools work together to create differentiated lessons, and then compile them into a school binder or online collection that others can use and learn from.

Not the end, but the Beginning...

I wish you well on your journey to differentiate by interest. I would wager that after trying a few lessons you will be hooked as you watch the engagement and responses of your students. My concluding thought is one of my favorite poems by John Steinbeck. I hope that for my students, I am one of these teachers.

Like Captured Fireflies

In her classroom our speculations

ranged the world

She aroused us to book waving discussion.

Every morning we came to her carrying new

truths, new facts, new ideas cupped

and sheltered in

our hands like captured fireflies.

When she went away a sadness

came over us,

But the light did not go out.

She left her signature upon us.

The literature of the teacher who

writes on children's minds.

I've had many teachers who taught

us soon forgotten things,

But only a few like her who created in me a new

thing, a new attitude, a new hunger.

I suppose that to a large extent I am the

unsigned manuscript of the teacher.

What deathless power lies in the hands

of such a person.

—John Steinbeck

Blackline Masters

Blackline Master 1:
Primary Student Interest Inventory

Name _____ Date_____

Circle the face that best describes how you feel about the following statements.

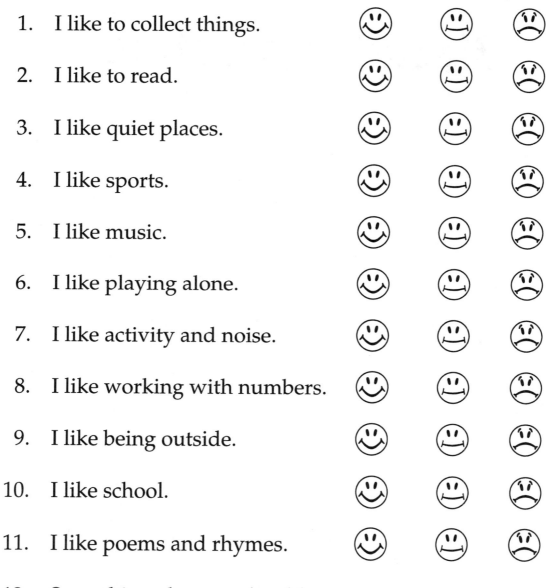

1. I like to collect things.

2. I like to read.

3. I like quiet places.

4. I like sports.

5. I like music.

6. I like playing alone.

7. I like activity and noise.

8. I like working with numbers.

9. I like being outside.

10. I like school.

11. I like poems and rhymes.

12. Something else you should
     know about me is

Blackline Master 2:
Elementary Student Interest Inventory

Name _____ Date _____

1. What are your hobbies? How much time do you spend on them?

2. What are your favorite TV shows? Why do you like them?

3. Tell about a vacation you would like to take or have taken?

4. How are you smart?

5. What is your favorite activity at school and why?

6. What do you think you might want to do as a career when you are an adult?

7. What kinds of books and magazines do you like?

8. Do you participate in sports or take lessons? What are they?

9. When you have free time at home, what do you like to do?

10. What is one thing you can do very well?

11. Who are your friends? Why are they your friends?

12. What else is important for people to know about you?

Blackline Master 3:
Nonverbal Interest Inventory

Name _____ Date _____

Instructions

1. Write your name in the oval.
2. In the space around the oval, draw or paste pictures that represent things that interest you. Include hobbies, sports, television programs, games, and so on.

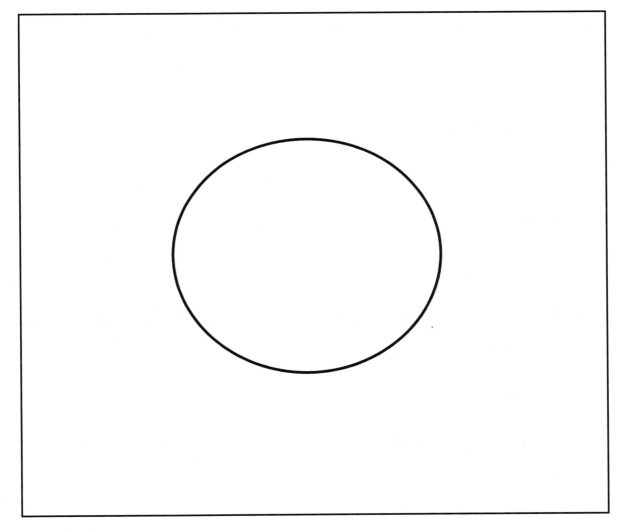

Variation

Paste a picture of the student in the center of the page.

Blackline Master 4:
Parent-Completed Student Interest Inventory

Dear Parents,

   The purpose of this inventory is to give a clear picture of some of your child's interests, so that we can capitalize on some of them over the course of the school year. Thank you for completing this survey. Please return to school by _____.

Yours truly,

---

1. What are your child's favorite subjects in school?

2. What subjects are your child's least favorite?

3. What are your child's interests outside of school?

4. What TV programs, movies, and books hold your child's interest?

5. When your child has free time, what does he or she choose to do?

6. What kinds of careers has your child expressed an interest in?

7. What kinds of things does your child like to learn about?

8. Describe how your child learns best (in a quiet place, with others, talking, etc.)

9. What else can you tell me about your child's interests and how he or she learns best?

10. What two words best describe your child?

_____   _____

Child's Name   Parent's Name

Blackline Master 5:
The Treasures of Me

Date

Dear Students,

This activity will help your classmates get to know you and what makes you unique.

1. Find a small box.
2. Write your name on the outside and decorate it if you wish.
3. Fill it with items that will let your classmates know about your interests. Consider things such as:

    - Pictures
    - Drawings
    - Souvenirs
    - Items from collections
    - Brochures
    - Toys/Hobbies
    - Trophies/Medals

Be creative! Think of things that could fit in the box that you can use to tell about your own unique interests. Your day to share "The Treasures of Me" is _____.
I'm looking forward to learning more about you!

Sincerely,

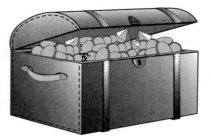

Blackline Master 6:
Interest Quilt Square

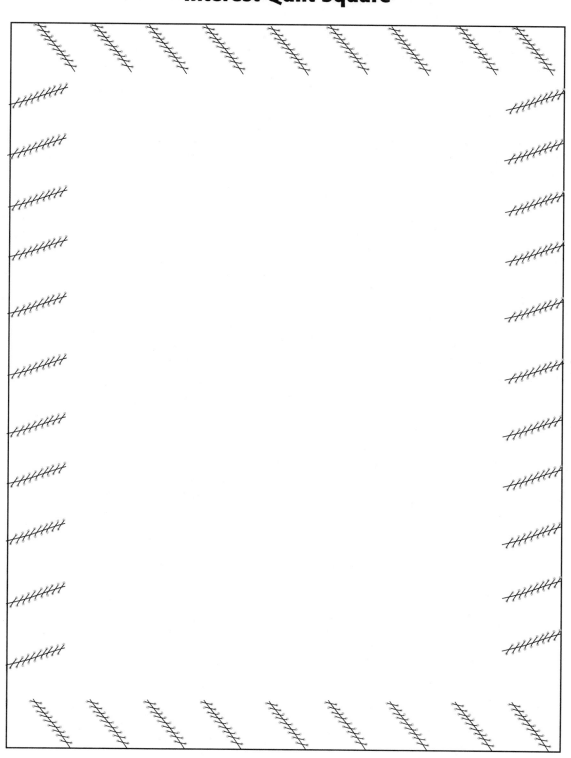

Blackline Master 7:
Venn Diagram Interest Interviews

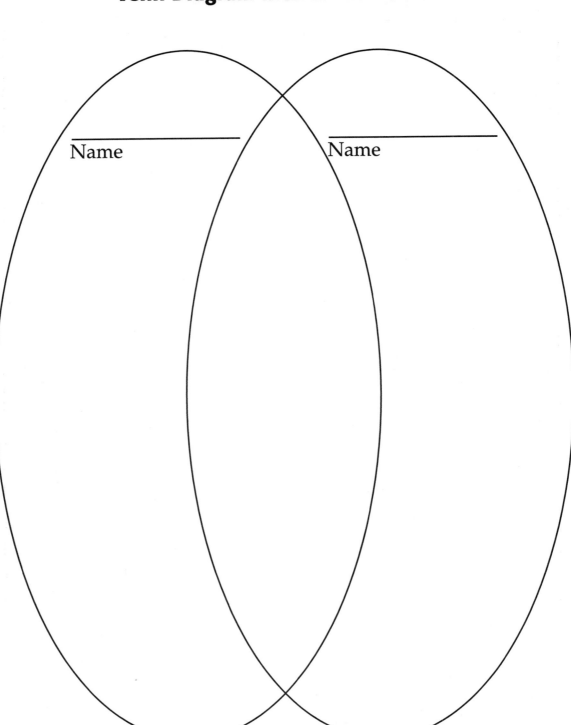

Name

Name

Blackline Master 8:
Triple Venn Diagram Interest Interviews

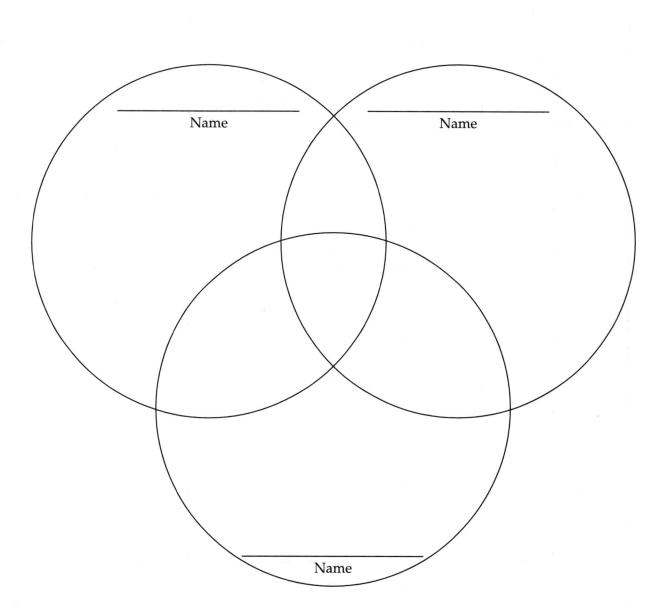

Blackline Master 9:
Interest Bar Graph

Blackline Master 10:
Puzzle Pieces

Individual Puzzle Template

Blackline Master 11:
Important Book

The important thing about me is _____

_____

_____

_____

_____

_____

But, the most important thing about me is _____

_____

_____

_____

_____

_____

_____

Blackline Master 12:
Another Important Book

The important thing about being _____

_____

_____

is that _____

_____

_____

_____

But, the most important thing about being _____

_____

_____

is that _____

_____

_____

_____

Blackline Master 13:
Ish Books/Posters

I am _____ -ish.

Blackline Master 14:
Interest Bingo

Blackline Master 15:
KUDo Quick Reference

Before we can effectively differentiate, we must be able to be able to articulate what the most important understandings are within a unit or an individual lesson. We must be clear on what we want students to know, understand, and be able to do. They should come directly from mandated standards and/or curriculum documents.

KUDo Component	Description	Key Question
Know	• Facts, definitions • Lower-level items on Bloom's taxonomy (**know**)	What content, facts, and definitions should students come to know as a result of this learning?
Understand	• Concepts, underlying principles • Higher-level tasks on Bloom's taxonomy (**comprehend, analysis, synthesis, evaluation**)	What concepts or principles should students be able to generalize and transfer and apply as a result of this learning?
Be able to **Do**	• Demonstration of learning • Similar to the **application** tasks on Bloom's taxonomy	What will the students do to demonstrate their learning?

Blackline Master 16:
Checklist for Creating a Choice Board

❐ Identify the KUDos—What do you want the students to know, understand, and be able to do?

❐ Brainstorm a variety of activities.

❐ Eliminate tasks that will not lead the students to these KUDos.

❐ Decide on what your choice board will look like. Will you create a tic-tac-toe, a list of choices, or a structure that matches a theme of study?

❐ How will you have students work through these tasks?

   ❑ Will you have one *core* activity that all students must complete to learn a key concept and then complete a vertical, horizontal, or diagonal line of other activities from there?

   ❑ Will you have a *free space* or *free choice* somewhere on the board where students can design their own activity?

❐ Choose the activities from your brainstormed list and place onto the board.

❐ Decide how the projects will be evaluated.

Blackline Master 17:
Checklist for Creating a RAFT Project

❏ Identify the KUDos—What do you want the student(s) to know, understand, and be able to do as a result of completing the RAFT project?

❏ Brainstorm a variety of projects the student(s) could complete (these will become the formats).

❏ Eliminate the tasks that will not lead the student(s) to what you want them to know, understand, and be able to do.

❏ Brainstorm roles, audiences, and topics for each format. Aim for things that would be interesting and engaging for students.

❏ Determine how the project(s) will be evaluated.

Blackline Master 18:
Generic Cube

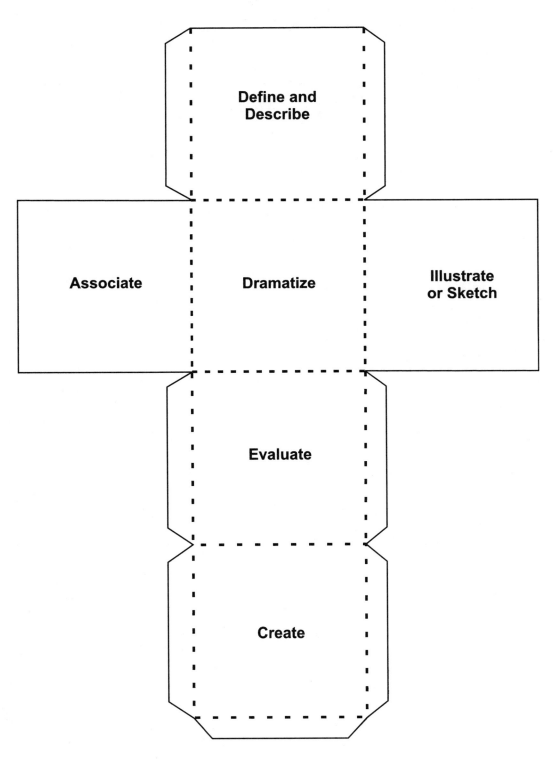

Define and
Describe

Associate

Dramatize

Illustrate
or Sketch

Evaluate

Create

Blackline Master 19: Blank Cube

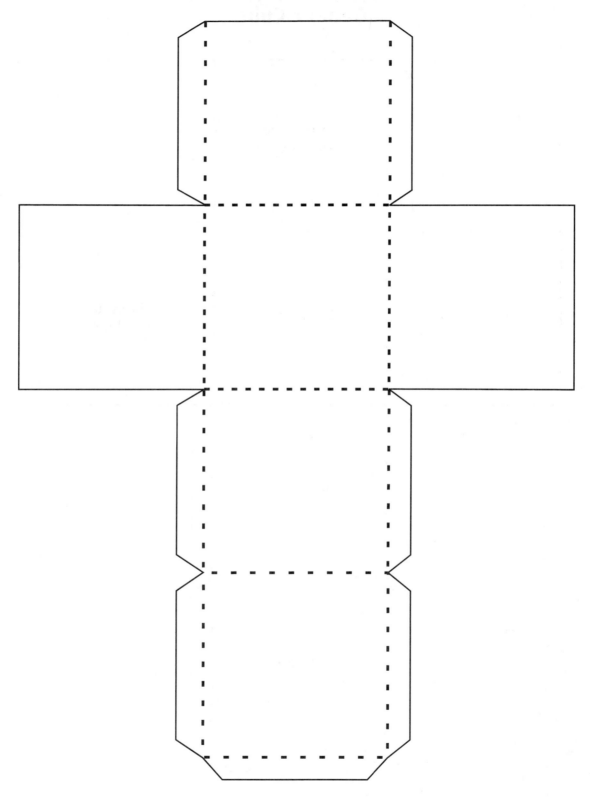

Blackline Master 20:
Checklist for Creating Cubing Project

❏ Identify the KUDos—What do you want the student(s) to know, understand, and be able to do as a result of completing the cubing activity?

❏ Brainstorm a variety of tasks the student(s) could complete.

❏ Eliminate the tasks that will not lead the student(s) to what you want them to know, understand, and be able to do.

❏ Choose the best six activities, so there is one for each face of the cube.

❏ Decide on a reasonable timeline to complete the task.

❏ Determine how the project(s) will be evaluated.

❏ Create the cube(s).

Blackline Master 21:
Checklist for Creating a Learning Contract

This process can be done by the teacher or in cooperation with a student or group of students.

❏ Identify the KUDos—What do you want the student(s) to know, understand, and be able to do as a result of completing the contract?

❏ Brainstorm a variety of tasks the student(s) could complete.

❏ Eliminate the tasks that will not lead the student(s) to what you want them to know, understand, and be able to do.

❏ Consider how the contract will be differentiated (by interest, readiness, or learning profile).

❏ Decide on a reasonable timeline to complete the tasks and how many students will be asked to complete it.

❏ Determine how and the frequency with you will check in with students during their contract work. Make this explicit in the contract.

❏ Outline how students will ask for help, if needed.

❏ List the resources that students are able to use, and how they should be cited.

❏ Determine how the project(s) will be evaluated. Give the rubrics or other evaluation tools to the students and discuss together before they start the assignment.

❏ Write up contract in a businesslike manner. Be sure to include places for dates and signatures.

Blackline Master 22:
Checklist for Creating a WebQuest

❏ Decide on a subject/topic.

❏ Identify the KUDos—What do you want students to know, understand, and be able to do as a result of completing the WebQuest?

❏ Brainstorm activity structures and tasks that would lead students to the important learning outcomes.

❏ Eliminate the tasks that will not lead the student(s) to what you want them to know, understand, and be able to do.

❏ Search for Web sites that are of an appropriate reading level and contain information that students will need.

❏ Choose tasks and Web sites that would most effectively lead students to understanding the important learning outcomes.

❏ Write guiding questions and step-by-step instructions for each task.

❏ Decide on an introduction or *hook* that will engage students in the task.

❏ Determine how students will present or share their information.

❏ Decide how student work will be evaluated.

Blackline Master 23:
Checklist for Planning a Lesson Differentiated by Interest

❐ Identify the subject and topic of study.

❐ Identify the KUDos—What the students should know, understand, and be able to do as a result of completing the activity.

❐ Decide on an activity structure that will allow students to choose a task that interests them (e.g., tic-tac-toe or other choice board, RAFT, WebQuest, learning contract etc.).

❐ Brainstorm activities that could possibly meet the learning outcomes.

❐ Eliminate the activities that will not lead the students to know, understand, and be able to do the important learning outcomes.

❐ Choose the activities that are the most engaging and will lead the students to the same learning outcomes.

❐ Describe the learning activities in detail. Create student handouts, if appropriate.

❐ Decide which parts of the activity will be assessed, and how they will be assessed.

❐ Determine how you will bring closure to the activities, and/or how you will facilitate the sharing of learning.

Blackline Master 24:
Differentiating by Interest

Lesson Plan Template

Subject:	Topic:

Outcomes

As a result of this study, students should:

Know:

Understand:

Be able to do:

Lesson Structure

☐ Choice board	☐ Learning contract
☐ RAFT	☐ Cubing
☐ WebQuest	☐ Other

Description of learning activities:

Assessment:

Closure/Sharing:

Blackline Master 25:
3-2-1 Exit Card

3 _____

2 _____

1 _____

. . . .

3 _____

2 _____

1 _____

Blackline Master 26: Generic Rubric

Category	4	3	2	1
Seek	• Uses a wide range of authentic and reliable resources • Information clearly relates to the main topic and includes an abundance of supporting details and/or examples • Evidence used is gathered from a wide variety of sources • Carefully and accurately logs research process • References are done appropriately and accurately	• Uses a range of authentic and reliable resources • Information relates to the main topic and includes many supporting details and/or examples • Evidence used is gathered from a variety of sources • Accurately logs research process • References are done accurately	• Uses some authentic and reliable resources • Information somewhat relates to the main topic and includes some supporting details and/or examples • Evidence used is limited, as is number of sources • Research process is logged in a limited way • References are complete but may contain errors	• Uses unreliable resources • Information does not relate to the main topic and includes few supporting details and/or examples • Evidence used is unclear, and limited number of sources used • Research process is not logged • References are incomplete or missing
Think	• Provides an insightful, comprehensive summary of the topic • Makes many unexpected and useful connections • Extremely logical development of ideas • Draws valid and well-supported conclusions	• Provides a complete summary of the topic • Makes some unexpected and useful connections • Logical development of ideas • Draws valid and supported conclusions	• Provides a partial summary of the topic • Makes some useful connections • Somewhat logical development of ideas • Draws valid conclusions that may not be well supported	• Provides vague information on the topic • Connections not easily seen • Ideas not logically developed • Conclusions false or unsupported
Self-Evaluate	• Is aware of and articulately talks about own thinking • Is extremely effective in evaluating own work	• Is aware of and talks about own thinking • Is effective in evaluating own work	• Is somewhat aware of and talks about own thinking • Is somewhat effective in evaluating own work	• Has difficulty in talking about own thinking • Is ineffective in evaluating own work

Blackline Master 27:
Thinking About Our Activity

Name _____

I understood the main idea.   😊   🙂   ☹️

I shared my thinking with others. 😊   🙂   ☹️

I listened to others.   😊   🙂   ☹️

Here is a question I still have

_____

_____

_____

_____

Blackline Master 28:
Project Reflection

Name
While doing this project, I did well with
While doing this project, it was difficult for me to
Next time, I will

Blackline Master 29:
Independent Study Self-Evaluation

Name _____ Date _____

What I did best:

What I would do differently next time:

Blackline Master 30:
Self-Evaluation

Name _____ Date _____

Circle the face that best describes how you feel about the following statements.

1. I enjoyed working on my project.

2. I used my time well.

3. I used different sources of information.

4. I organized my information.

5. I am proud of my final product.

The things I would most like you to notice about my work on this project are:

_____

_____

_____

_____

Blackline Master 31: Goal Setting

Photocopy this page and the next page on a single paper, back-to-back.

1.   Write your goal(s) in the space below.

2.   Fold in half, tape together, and address to yourself (use the back of this page).

3.   Fill in "open on" to a date where you would like to check your progress.

My goal(s) to improve _____is/are:

_____

_____

_____

I will accomplish this goal by

_____

_____

_____

_____
Signature

To: _____

Open on: _____

Blackline Master 32:
Project Log

What I worked on/completed:	What I still need to do:
I need:	Evaluation of my work time:

What I worked on/completed:	What I still need to do:
I need:	Evaluation of my work time:

Blackline Master 33:
Pathway to an Independent Project

Name _____

1. Start date: _____

Due date: _____

2. Choose a topic.

3. Make a plan page for completing your project.

4. Share your plan with your teacher.

5. Gather materials and resources to do your project.

6. Find and organize your information.

7. Choose a way to share your project.

8. Present your project to your classmates.

9. Discuss your project with your teacher.

10. Complete a self evaluation.

11. Congratulations! You did it!

Blackline Master 34:
Goal Setting

1. Set your goal(s) for differentiating your instruction in the space below.

2. Fold in half, tape together, and address to yourself (use the back of this page).

3. Fill in "open on" to a date where you would like to check your progress (e.g., one month from today, three months from today—whatever you feel is doable).

4. Tape shut and then tape into your plan book on the date that you want to check your progress.

A goal I have to move ahead in differentiating my instruction is

_____

_____

_____

_____

_____

I will accomplish this goal by

_____

_____

_____

_____

_____

Signature

To: _____

Open on: _____

Annotated Webliography

Ripple Effect Learning: Available at http://rippleeffectlearning.com/

This is my little home on the Web. Click on "Resources" to find links to resources such as checklists, lesson plans, and Blackline Masters.

Differentiated Instruction Hotlist (Falmouth Public Schools): Available at http://www.kn.sbc.com/wired/fil/pages/listdifferensp.html

This is a list created by teachers with links to differentiated instruction (DI) sites.

CAST Differentiated Instruction: Available at http://www.cast.org/publications/ncac/ncac_diffinstruc.html#download

This is the Center for Applied Special Technology's site on DI. It contains basic information on DI references and downloads and annotated links to other sites.

LEADERS Project: Available at http://www.education.pitt.edu/leaders/ FAQ/differentiatedinstruc.htm

You will find DI resources, strategies, and ideas through a project by Pittsburgh educators.

Differentiated Instruction: Available at http://tst1160-35.k12.fsu.edu/ mainpage.html

This site has links to ideas, resources, and lesson plans by Leon County Schools.

Welcome to Differentiated Instruction: Available at http://web.west bloomfield.k12.mi. us/ealy/lafer/

This is a nicely organized site by West Bloomfield Schools with resources for teachers, parents, and students.

Staff Development for Educators: Available at http://differentiatedinstruction.com/?c1=partner&source=TeacherNet&Pro_Resources

Click on the Differentiated Instruction Resource page link for downloadable ideas and documents.

Differentiated Instruction—A Scavenger Hunt: Available at http://www.frsd.k12.nj.us/rfmslibrarylab/di/background.htm

You will find an Internet scavenger hunt that might be useful in a staff development or sharing session.

Internet4Classrooms: Differentiated Instruction: Available at http://www.internet4classrooms. com/di.htm

This site has quite an extensive list of links divided into sections: instructional theory, practical tips for the classroom, sample units and lessons multilink sites, and other resources.

Instructional and Management Strategies: Available at http://www.mcps. k12.md.us/curriculum/enriched/giftedprograms/instructionalstrategy.shtm

You will find a nice set of links and information on topics such as anchor activities, compacting tiering, and learning contracts including PowerPoint presentations.

Teachnology Tutorial: How to Differentiate Instruction: Available at http://www.teach-nology.com/tutorials/teaching/differentiate/planning

This site provides a collection of information on the following topics: how to plan for differentiated instruction, direct instruction, inquiry-based learning, cooperative learning, information processing strategies, instructional activities, and assessment.

Enhancing Learning with Technology: Differentiated Instruction: Available at http://members.shaw.ca/priscillatheroux/differentiating.html

You will find a wealth of links to basic information, learning strategies, teacher resources, sample lesson plans, and more.

About Differentiated Instruction: Available at http://faculty.rmwc.edu/mentor_grant/Differentiated/differentiated_instruction.htm

There are links to lesson plans and strategies from Randolph-Macon Woman's College.

From Now On: Scaffolding for Success: Available at http://fno.org/dec99/scaffold.html

This is an article on scaffolding, including links to practical examples.

Tools for Schools: Differentiated Instruction: Available at http://www.emsc.nysed.gov/ciai/sate/resourcesdiffinstr.pdf

This is an excellent document that helps teachers to self-assess where they are with DI as well as provides ideas for strategies.

A Different Place: Available at http://adifferentplace.org/teachers.htm

Although this is a resource designed for gifted education, it offers some good information on DI and on reaching learners who need a challenge.

Technology Tip

Effective Searching

You may want to continue to search on your own because resources are constantly evolving. Try using quotes around your search terms to ensure that they appear together on a Web page (e.g., "differentiated instruction").

References

Alexander, P. A., Kulikowich, J. M., & Jetton, T. L. (1994, Summer). The role of subject-matter knowledge and interest in the processing of linear and nonlinear texts. *Review of Educational Research, 64*(2), 201–252.

Bergin, D. A. (1999, Spring). Influences on classroom interest. *Educational Psychologist, 34*(2), 87–98.

Brophy, J. (1999, Spring). Toward a model of the value aspects of motivation in education: Developing an appreciation for particular learning domains and activities. *Educational Psychologist, 34*(2), 75–86.

Chapman C., & King, R. (2005). *Differentiated assessment strategies: One tool doesn't fit all.* Thousand Oaks, CA: Corwin Press Inc.

Deci, E. L., Vallerand, R. J., Pelletier, L. G., & Ryan, R. M. (1991). Motivation and education: The self-determination perspective. *Educational Psychologist, 26*(3 & 4), 325–346.

Dodge, B. (1997). Some thoughts about WebQuests. The WebQuest Page. Retrieved April 15, 2004 from http://edweb.sdsu.edu/courses/edtec596/about_ webquests.html.

Ediger, M. (2005). How to generate student excitement in science. *Science Activities, 41*(4), 15–17.

Heacox, D. (2002). *Differentiated instruction in the regular classroom: How to reach and teach all learners, grades 3-12.* Minneapolis, MN: Free Spirit Publishing.

Ishee, J. H. (2005, January). The effect of choice on motivation. *Journal of Physical Education, Recreation & Dance, 76*(1), 8.

Kohn, A. (September, 1993). Choices for children: Why and how to let students decide. *Phi Delta Kappan, 75*(1), 18–21.

Lause, J. (2004). Using reading workshop to inspire lifelong readers. *English Journal, 93*(5), 24–30.

Mandel Morrow, L. (2004). Motivation: The forgotten factor. *Reading Today, 21*(5), 6.

Santa, C. (1988). *Content reading including study systems.* Dubuque, IA: Kendall/Hunt Publishing.

Scherer, M. (2002, September). Do students care about learning: A conversation with Mihaly Csikszentmihalyi. *Educational Leadership, 60*(1), 12–17.

Schraw, G., Flowerday, T., & Lehman, S. (2001). Increasing situational interest in the classroom. *Educational Psychology Review, 13*(3), 211–224.

Stone, S. J. (1995). Empowering teachers, empowering children. *Childhood Education, 71*(5), 294–296.

Strong, R., Silver, H., Perini, M., & Tuculescu, G., (2003, September). Boredom and its opposite. *Educational Leadership, 61*(1), 24–29.

Stronge, J. H. (2002). *Qualities of effective teachers.* Alexandria, VA: Association for Supervision and Curriculum Development.

Todd, C. (1995). The semester project: The power and pleasures of independent study. *English Journal, 84*(3), 74–77.

Tomlinson, C. A. (2001). *How to differentiate instruction in mixed-ability classrooms.* Alexandria VA: Association for Supervision and Curriculum Development.

Tomlinson, C. A. (2004, August). Research evidence for differentiation. *School Administrator, 61*(7), 30.

Tomlinson, C. A., & Demirsky Allan, S. (2000). *Leadership for differentiating schools & classrooms.* Alexandria, VA: Association for Supervision and Curriculum Development.

Wormeli, R. (March, 2005). Busting myths about differentiated instruction. *Principal Leadership, 5*(7), 28–33.

Wormeli, R. (2006). *Fair isn't always equal: Assessing & grading in the differentiated classroom.* Portland, ME: Stenhouse Publishers.